The Illustrated Encyclopedia of
CIVIL WAR
COLLECTIBLES

*A Comprehensive Guide to Union and Confederate
Arms, Equipment, Uniforms, and Other Memorabilia*

CHUCK LAWLISS

An Owl Book
Henry Holt and Company
New York

Henry Holt and Company, Inc.
Publishers since 1866
115 West 18th Street
New York, New York 10011

Henry Holt ® is a registered trademark of
Henry Holt and Company, Inc.

Library of Congress Catalog Card Number 97-70769

ISBN 0-8050-4635-6

Henry Holt books are available for special promotions
and premiums. For details contact: Director, Special Markets.

First Edition—1997

Produced by Wieser & Wieser, Inc.
Designed by Tony Meisel

Printed in the United States of America
All first editions are printed on acid-free paper. ∞

10 9 8 7 6 5 4 3 2 1

The technical consultant for this book, J. Craig Nanos, is a lieutenant colonel in the Pennsylvania Army Reserve National Guard and a Fellow in the Company of Military Historians. His company, The Sentry Post, has designed and constructed exhibits for such clients as the West Point Museum and the National Park Service. He has also created uniforms and equipment for motion pictures, including *Last of the Mohicans, A Midnight Clear,* and *Taps.* Mr. Nanos, who makes his home in the Philadelphia area, has collected Civil War memorabilia for many years.

CONTENTS

PHOTO CREDITS

INTRODUCTION

People were collecting Civil War artifacts and memorabilia even before the Civil War had ended. Soldiers on both sides exchanged buttons, badges, canteens, and insignia. Soldiers were always looking for souvenirs, not only from the battlefield but also from public buildings and private homes. They sent traded, captured, or confiscated items home to family and friends and brought more home when they were mustered out

Contemporary accounts describe the citizens of Gettysburg searching the battlefield for firearms, swords, shells, musket balls, uniforms, buttons, blankets, harnesses, and personal effects—anything that would serve as a memento of the great battle. Many of these artifacts would be sold to the people who came later to see the battlefield site. So there were dealers as well as collectors from the very beginning.

Few families, North or South, were untouched by the events of the war. Parents, wives, and friends saved letters from their soldiers and displayed daguerreotypes and artifacts from the war. Even today, Civil War mementos are being rediscovered in family attics. In recent times, countless metal items have been recovered from battlefields by enthusiasts using metal detectors.

The assassination of President Abraham Lincoln was a stimulus to collectors. Grief-stricken mourners sought prints, broadsides, and newspaper and magazine accounts of the deathbed scene, the funeral train back to Springfield, and the capture and punishment of John Wilkes Booth and his co-conspirators.

The Centennial Exposition in 1876 and the Colombian Exposition of 1893 rekindled interest in the country's historic heritage. Chromolithography made possible inexpensive mass-produced broadsides, trade cards, posters, framed prints, and wall hangings. Scenes of battles and Civil War personalities sold by the millions. Few Southern homes were without a colored reproduction of "The Last Meeting" of Confederate Generals Robert E. Lee and Stonewall Jackson.

Like the expositions of the late 1800s, something was always coming along to stimulate interest in the Civil War. In the 1930s, it was *Gone with the Wind*. In the 1960s, it was the centennial of the war. In the 1990s, it was Ken Burns's PBS documentary *The Civil War*. Newspapers reported that the documentary, which was seen by more than 15 million people, had caused the prices for Civil War collectibles to rise an average of 25 percent.

Reenactors at Fredericksburg fire a volley, graphically demonstrating why soldiers had trouble seeing the enemy on the battlefield before the invention of smokeless powder. Reenactors demand authenticity in their uniforms and equipment, and many enthusiasts who can't afford the real thing now collect items made for reenactors. (NPS)

An editor of *American Heritage* magazine once observed: "There has never been a revival of interest in the Civil War, because it has never gone away." Indeed, the Civil War was the great watershed event in American history, and even today, it continues to sustain a sense of immediacy and reality.

An estimated 250,000 Americans describe themselves as Civil War hobbyists. They may belong to Civil War organizations, take part in reenactments of the war, read Civil War periodicals and books, join Civil War round tables, or collect items that were somehow involved in the war. The war is a real part of their lives.

Collecting Civil War memorabilia covers a wide spectrum, from buying a Minie ball for a dollar in a tourist shop to buying a Confederate battle flag for $75,000 at a Lancaster County, Pennsylvania, auction house. This book concentrates on the middle range, objects that cost from a hundred dollars to a few thousand.

This is the price range for most serious collectors, those people who care about the war, want to know more about the war, and see collecting as part of that experience. On one end of the spectrum, this book ignores those who want only a souvenir of a visit to a Civil War battlefield. On the other end, it ignores those who see rare Civil War artifacts primarily as an investment and part of a portfolio.

This is not to suggest that there's anything wrong with looking at Civil War memorabilia as an investment. A collector who buys intelligently will find it is a good investment. Good Civil War memorabilia have increased steadily in value over the past several decades at a rate that has exceeded that of blue-chip stocks.

But a serious collector also buys with passion. Buying a Spencer carbine or a Lee autograph is a more emotional experience than buying soybean futures or stock in a chemical company.

Most serious Civil War collectors specialize. Most, in one way or another, personalize the war. A doctor may collect the instruments of wartime surgeons. A black social worker may seek out material from black regiments. A stockbroker may decorate his office with bond certificates issued by the Confederacy to finance the war. A weekend sailor may love prints and paintings of blockade-runners and Confederate privateers. A banker may love her Uncle Sam mechanical bank, and the house of the headmistress of a fashionable girls' school may be filled with toys and games of the period. A fashion photographer may have an important collection of cartes de visite and daguerreotypes, while a literary critic may specialize in first editions of war memoirs.

This book is designed to help collectors in several ways. First, it provides an overview of the mechanics of the Civil War—what the various components of the military were and how they did what they did.

Second, it discusses in detail and illustrates the major items of the war—firearms, edged weapons, uniforms, and accouterments—as well as many of the minor items. Included within this alphabetical listing of collectibles are a number of terms that may be of interest to collectors.

Third, the book reports the price ranges that specific items have commanded at recent auctions.

Fourth, in the appendixes, it presents a variety of information useful to beginning collectors—a representative sample of Civil War auction houses and dealers; lists of Civil War organizations, museums, and periodicals; and suggestions on how to become a savvy collector and how to care for your Civil War artifacts.

This book, however, can serve only as a guide; the field is simply too large and prices too volatile for any book to be definitive. But to a true collector, the very size and volatility of the field simply make collecting that much more interesting.

Experienced collectors know that a number of factors affect the worth of Civil War artifacts and memorabilia. The worth of a piece is directly related to its rarity. This is the major reason why Confederate items fetch considerably more than comparable Union items. And the rarer the piece, the more volatile the price.

The condition of a collectible is another important factor. No artifact that survived a war some 130 years ago will be in pristine condition, but the range of conditions is wide. Some collectors value condition more than rarity, although if a piece is in excellent condition, it may indicate that it never was

Many a Confederate soldier brought a slave with him when he went to war to do the chores of army life. In camp, a banjo-playing slave entertained his master, General J. E. B. Stuart. Slave labor battalions built entrenchments around Richmond, and late in the war, the Confederate Congress debated offering freedom to slaves who would fight as soldiers. (NA)

used in battle. Examine a piece carefully before buying. Look not only for flaws but also for modern repairs and to see if the piece is a reproduction.

Affiliation with a particular personality, unit, or event also affects price. Anything belonging to a well-known general will be expensive. A canteen carried by a soldier in the Stonewall Brigade will be worth a lot more than an ordinary Confederate canteen. Similarly, a rifle fired at Gettysburg has an enhanced worth.

In some instances, prices will carry the designation "E" or "NE." This refers to whether the piece was excavated or not (dug or nondug). Excavated pieces, or more accurately, what is left of them, are found on battlefields and at campsites, usually by metal detectors. An excavated piece saw action, while many nonexcavated pieces never left the armory or warehouse. Some collectors specialize in excavated pieces, and many excavated pieces command high prices.

The items listed in this book represent a relatively small sampling of items commonly available from dealers or at auction. The prices listed were chosen to represent average dealer prices; otherwise, the price represents that received at a recent auction. It is important to remember, however, that prices are in a constant state of flux, and an average price when this book was written may not be an average price when you go to buy.

BRANCHES OF SERVICE

The structures of the Union and Confederate armies were markedly similar, which was understandable because the great majority of senior officers in both armies were trained at the U.S. Military Academy at West Point. General Robert E. Lee, for example, not only was a graduate but had been superintendent of the academy before the war. Lee's president, Jefferson Davis, was a West Pointer, and so was Lee's nemesis, General Ulysses S. Grant, as were most of the other Union commanders Lee faced. Many of the military textbooks at West Point, such as Rifle and Light Infantry Tactics, *were written by William Joseph Hardee, who later cast his lot with the Confederacy. This similarity of structure makes it useful to first examine the various branches of the armies and the equipment peculiar to those branches, then to note the differences the circumstances of the war forced on both sides.*

ARTILLERY

The artillery of both armies was divided into field artillery and heavy artillery. Field artillery was ordnance sufficiently light and mobile to move with the army in the field and to be used in battle. Field artillery also included mountain artillery, exceptionally light equipment that could be transported in pieces on the back of a mule. Heavy artillery included siege guns and siege mortars, which, if mobile, were unwieldy and slow; garrison or fortress artillery; and the great coastal cannons like the huge Rodmans, the largest of which weighed 117,000 pounds and fired a 1,080-pound projectile 8,000 yards.

Ordnance was also divided into types. Guns were comparatively heavy, of long range and flat trajectory, and they were smoothbore and fired solid shot. Howitzers were lighter and shorter and fired a relatively heavy shell with a light charge. Mortars were very short and heavy and fired large projectiles with a high trajectory. Both howitzers and mortars also were smoothbores.

The lighter smoothbore ordnance was usually of bronze, although often referred to as brass. Some rifled pieces were made of bronze, but the rifling wore out rapidly. Most rifled field pieces were made of cast iron, some with wrought-iron reinforcing hoops at the breech. The large smoothbore tubes used in fixed positions were nearly all made of cast iron.

Cast iron could be produced easily and cheaply but was comparatively weak and brittle and not up to the strain of firing with heavy charges in a rifled gun. Steel was superior but expensive and difficult to produce and work in large quantities.

Nearly all Civil War guns were muzzleloaders. Field artillery could be loaded "down the spout" as fast as, if not faster than, a gun crew could operate the relatively clumsy and complicated breech mechanisms then in use.

Civil War guns had no recoil mechanisms. When fired, they leaped back in recoil and had to be run back into position and reaimed after each round.

Fuses were uncertain, and many failed to ignite or ignited prematurely. Even when they ignited properly, Civil War shells were far less destructive than modern projectiles of the same caliber.

The walls of the shells were thick, and bursting charges were small, so that missiles broke into a few large pieces, with a low velocity. Elongated projectiles for rifled guns held more powder, and some types were scored internally to ensure better fragmentation.

Many rifle shells, however, were fitted with impact fuses. On hitting the

Blockade-runners brought British-made Whitworths to the Confederacy. It was one of the few successful breech-loading cannons of its time. (NA)

ground, they often buried themselves before exploding, thus reducing their efficiency. The effect of such fire against infantry under cover was so slight that long-range cannonading was looked upon scornfully by veteran troops.

The field artilleryman's most lethal load was canister. The tin cylinders filled with iron shot or musket balls turned a cannon into a huge shotgun. Against troops in mass formation at short range, canister was devastating and undoubtedly caused more casualties than all other artillery projectiles combined.

To use canister, a gunner had to bring his piece into action well within range of enemy riflemen. If there were sharpshooters, this was suicide. Although batteries often were galloped up to close range to unlimber amid a hail of bullets, it was considered a sacrificial move, to be made only in moments of dire necessity and at an inevitably high cost in men and horses.

The rifled musket changed the role of the field gun from an assault weapon to a support weapon. The infantry usually attacked unshaken by effective preliminary bombardment.

Many guns were installed in permanent fortifications. The defenses of Washington, D.C., alone contained 807 guns and 98 mortars. Most permanently installed guns never fired a shot at the enemy during the entire war.

Field guns were grouped in batteries. Six was considered the ideal number of guns in a battery, although four-gun batteries were common, especially in the Confederate army. The battery commander was usually a captain. A battery was composed of sections. Two guns formed a section, commanded by a lieutenant.

When troops were on the march, each gun, or piece, was hooked up behind a limber, which carried an ammunition chest and was drawn by six horses. Each piece had its own caisson, carrying three ammunition chests, and was drawn by a six-horse team. These two units made a platoon, commanded by a sergeant, who was the chief of piece, and two corporals.

Each battery was accompanied by a traveling forge, a battery wagon carrying tents and supplies, and usually six more caissons carrying reserve ammunition. Extra wagons for fodder and other supplies might be attached as necessary.

Confederate riflemen prepare to fire a volley at a reenactment in Corinth, Mississippi. When Civil War soldiers began using the new rifle-musket the advantage in battle switched to the defense, as many generals, North and South, learned to their sorrow. (CT)

In the horse artillery (also called the flying artillery), the cannoneers each rode a horse. Two additional men acted as horse holders in action. A lieutenant commanded the line of caissons. In addition, there were two staff sergeants (orderly and quartermaster), five artificers (who kept the pieces in good order), two buglers, and a guidon-bearer.

Four batteries were assigned to a division. When several divisions were organized into a corps, at least half the divisional artillery was grouped as a corps reserve. An army had a reserve of some 100 guns. The horse artillery was often attached to the cavalry corps or placed in the army reserve.

Until 1863, the Confederate army and the western army of the Union assigned a battery to each infantry brigade. This was a poor system, dispersing the guns throughout the army and making it difficult to concentrate artillery fire.

No set standard for the composition of the individual battery existed in either army. At the outbreak of war, a six-gun battery usually included two howitzers. A 12-pounder battery had four 12-pounder guns and two 24-pounder howitzers. A 6-pounder battery had four 6-pounder guns and two 12-pounder howitzers when available. The 6-pounder was used mostly by the South and was later replaced almost entirely by 3-inch rifles and 12-pounder smoothbores.

Opinions differed among artillerymen as to the relative merits of smoothbore and rifled cannons. One Confederate chief of ordnance said, "We especially valued the 3-inch rifles, which became the favorite field piece."

Rifled guns were of longer range and far greater accuracy. While there were some remarkable instances of "sharpshooting" with smoothbores, windage, irregular flight, and loss of velocity of the spherical missile made accurate shooting at any great distance impossible.

In wooded and broken country, however, it was seldom possible to place rifled guns where their long rang might be used to advantage. And the dense volumes of black-powder smoke made gun laying difficult, the direction sometimes marked only by the tracks made by the wheels in recoil.

The most popular fieldpiece was the Napoleon Model 1857, a 12-pounder gun-howitzer that could be fired from two to four times a minute. Although

Part of the job of an artilleryman was to help place cannons in advantageous places to fire on the enemy. These men are moving a field howitzer into place with the sweat of their brows. Later, they will bring up the ammunition. A gun crew consisted of nine men, and the gun was pulled by a team of six horses, except in cases like this. (NA)

A five-man gun crew goes through a simulated firing drill while their officers observe the performance. The soldier at left sponges out the barrel, using water from the leather bucket seen below the gun. Many steps are necessary to load and ready a gun for firing, and they must be performed smoothly and sequentially in the heat of battle for the gun to be effective. (NA)

it was a smoothbore cannon, the Napoleon was very effective at short range. The rifled cannon, because of greater range and accuracy, was especially effective against such large masonry fortifications as Fort Sumter. The most popular rifled cannons were the Parrott and the Rodman. Breechloaders also were used, most of them imported from England. Among these were the famous Whitworth as well as the Blakeley and the Armstrong.

Guns and howitzers took their denominations from the weight of their solid shot in round numbers, including the 42-pounder. Larger pieces, rifled guns, and mortars took their denominations from the diameter of the bore.

Field artillery ranged from 6- to 32-pounders in smoothbores and from the 2.56-inch Wiard, a 6-pounder, to the 3-inch types in rifles.

Siege and garrison artillery ranged from 4.2- to 10-inch pieces, while seacoast artillery ranged from the 5-inch 80-pounder Whitworth rifle to the 15-inch Columbiad. The largest of the seacoast cannons had a 20-inch bore; however, this huge cannon saw little or no actual service. The largest cannons most used were probably the 15-inch Columbiad and such pieces as the 300-pounder Parrott and the 13-inch mortar. Maximum ranges of Civil War siege cannons were 7,700 yards for the 80-pounder Whitworth rifle; 4,200 yards for the 10-inch mortar; and 4,300 yards for the 13-inch mortar.

Federal army cannons may be classified by the type of bore, by the method of loading, and by the type of trajectory.

The prewar smoothbores were gradually replaced by the new 12-pounder, or Napoleon, as it was familiarly called. This was a gun-howitzer of about 1,200 pounds with a diameter of 4.62 inches, whose projectiles were spherical solid shot, case shot, shell, and canister. The ammunition was all "fixed," in that the powder charge was attached to the projectile.

The first really effective use of rifled cannons was in 1862 at the siege operations at Fort Pulaski, near Savannah. Using 10 rifles and 26 smoothbores, Union artillery, firing from a mile away, breached the 7½-foot-thick brick walls in a bombardment that lasted barely 24 hours. The next year, Fort Sumter was recaptured using 100-, 200-, and 300-pounder Parrott rifles. The range and accuracy of these rifles startled the military world. A 30-pounder (4.2-inch) Parrott had an amazing carry of 8,453 yards with 800-pound hollow shot.

The rifled field guns most used were the 10-pounder (2.9-inch) Parrott and the regulation wrought-iron 3-inch gun. The range at the maximum 12- to 13-degree elevation was from 3,000 to 3,500 yards, or about 1¾ to 2 miles. With higher elevations, experienced artillerists could obtain ranges of up to 6,000 yards, or 3¼ miles.

A few of the larger rifled cannons became famous, including the "Swamp Angel" and "Whistling Dick." The former was an 8-inch 200-pounder Parrott rifle located on Morris Island. The city of Charleston, 7,900 yards from the piece, was its target. Union artillery fired 16 shells on the city on August 22, 1863. Twelve were of Parrott's construction and were filled with a fluid composition; the other four were filled with "Short's Solidified Greek Fire." After the war the "Swamp Angel" was sent to Trenton, New Jersey, to be melted but was identified and was set on a granite monument.

"Whistling Dick," a rifled Confederate 18-pounder, was made at the Tredegar Foundry, near Richmond, and was used in the defense of Vicksburg. Its projectiles gave off a peculiar whistling sound in their flight.

Cannons may be designated as guns, howitzers, or mortars, depending on whether the trajectories are relatively flat, medium, or high. The flat-trajectory guns usually had higher muzzle velocities than the other types. A gun usually had a smaller caliber than a howitzer or a mortar that fired the same weight of projectile, but because of its length and the thickness of its breech, the gun usually was heavier.

Howitzers usually were of larger caliber than guns, but they lobbed projectiles higher and had a shorter range. They were effective against enemy personnel positioned behind shelter or a hill.

Columbiads were a special large-caliber type of howitzer used for throwing solid shot, shells, spherical case, and canister.

Mortars were short-tube weapons of large caliber, used for crushing fortifications or setting fire to them. The weight of the projectile, rather than its velocity, produced the desired effect.

Mortar projectiles were formidable. The 12-inch mortar fired a 200-pound shell. During the siege of Petersburg, the Union used the "Dictator," which required special beds and a pair of rollers. In spite of their high trajectory, mortars could send a projectile considerably more than a mile.

CAVALRY

At the beginning of the war, the Confederate cavalry was unmatched in quality and leadership. To most Southern men, the horse was a part of everyday life. The landed gentry were all hard riders, and from this group, came the Confederate cavalry officers. The top echelons of the Confederate command had an affinity for the cavalry and felt comfortable employing it in battle. From the beginning, the Confederate cavalry was handled in large bodies with great skill and daring.

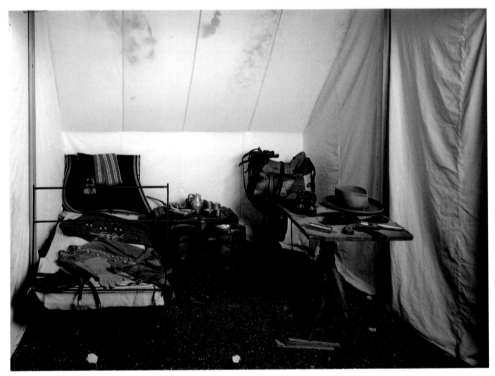

General Lee's personal possessions are displayed in a mock-up of a field tent at the Museum of the Confederacy in Richmond. Behind the bed, which Lee used during the siege of Petersburg, is a saddle blanket used on Lee's horse Traveler and a sash sent to Lee by an English admirer. The frock coat on the bed may have been worn by Lee at Appomattox. The frock coat at the foot of the bed was a gift from ladies in Maryland. By the bed is a mess chest and equipment and Lee's boots. The saddle is a modified Grimsley saddle, used by most Confederate generals. The table was used at Lee's winter headquarters near Orange Courthouse, Virginia. On it are his field glasses, hat, an engraved Colt Model 1851 Navy revolver, and the pen used to sign the surrender at Appomattox. (MOC)

Many Northern recruits had never been on a horse, which put the Union cavalry at a great disadvantage. While an infantryman could be sent into battle with a minimum of training, a cavalryman could not. A trooper who was more fearful of his horse than of the enemy was a distinct liability, and to place such men within reach of an aggressive enemy was to invite disaster.

In the first two years of the war, the Confederate cavalry rode rings around almost any Federal command—capturing its patrols, looting its wagon trains, burning its bridges, and escaping practically unharmed.

The Union cavalry learned its lessons. At the cost of many men and horses, the Union gradually developed units of cavalry that could give a good account of themselves. But no attempt was made to use Federal cavalry en masse as a separate striking force until General Joseph Hooker organized the cavalry of the Army of the Potomac into a corps. Assembled in a corps, these cavalrymen improved rapidly. Always better equipped than the Confederate cavalry, the Union cavalry eventually became its equal, then its superior. After the war, a member of Confederate General J. E. B. Stuart's staff said: "During the last two years no branch of the Army of the Potomac contributed to the overthrow of Lee's army as [did] the cavalry . . . . "

The strength of the Confederate cavalry declined as the war went on. Battle and disease took their tool, disabling both horses and men, and both were becoming increasingly difficult to replace. Under the Confederate system, troopers provided their own mounts and were paid for their use, as well as for their value if killed in action. But no compensation was made for horses lost during the hardships of campaign. Consequently, as horses became scarcer and more expensive, hundreds of troopers were unable to obtain mounts. Late in the war, the Confederate government supplied some horses but not enough to make a significant difference in the performance of the Confederate cavalry.

An additional handicap was the inability of the Confederate government to supply its cavalrymen with good weapons and accouterments. Much Federal equipment was captured but not enough of it to close the gap. While the Confederate cavalry was losing numbers and efficiency, the Union cavalry was gaining both.

The cavalry was traditionally the "eyes" of the army. The cavalry leader kept his commander-in-chief informed of the enemy's movements and also screened the movements of his own army from enemy patrols. Besides guarding the army's flanks, the cavalry acted as a mobile striking force. Whenever possible, it struck and destroyed enemy communications, supply lines, and railroad trains.

As the war progressed, this work was undertaken by forces involving thousands of men and horses. This created problems. Sometimes the great cavalry raids were made at a sacrifice in men and horses disproportionate to the results. And there was the danger that, when needed most, the cavalry would be away on some enterprise of its own. This happened at Gettysburg, when Stuart's cavalry did not arrive to join General Lee until the third day.

On the march, cavalry could cover some 35 miles in 8 hours without undue strain on men or horses. Much longer rides were made, however. During the Chambersburg raid in 1862, Confederate General Jubel Early's command rode 82 miles in 27 hours. On General John Hunt Morgan's great raid, his Confederate troopers once rode 90 miles in 35 hours.

Cavalry on the move took up a considerable amount of road. On Union General Philip H. Sheridan's great march before the Battle of Yellow Tavern, the huge column of some 10,000 troopers in three divisions and six batteries stretched for 13 miles. At a walk, cavalry could cover 4 miles an hour; at a slow trot, 6; at a maneuvering trot, 8; and at a full gallop, 16.

Troopers fought dismounted in various circumstances: to seize and hold ground until the arrival of the infantry; to force defended places not accessible to mounted troops; to fill gaps in a line of battle; or to cover a retreat. In action, one trooper in four served as a horse holder, keeping the mounts as close as possible to the firing line.

On both sides, supplying horses for the cavalry, for the artillery, and for wagons posed a formidable supply and logistics problem. The Federal government spent an estimated $124 million on horses during the war. With the average price of a horse at $150, the Union army used about 825,000 horses during the war.

The Union cavalry benefited from a system of remount depots At the

At the reenactment of the Battle of Antietam, members of the famed Stonewall Brigade prepare for action. Actually, A. P. Hill's brigade saved the day for Lee, arriving after a forced march from Harpers Ferry and without a pause, smashing the Union line. (CT)

depots, troopers were trained, newly purchased horses were received, and sick or injured horses were allowed to recuperate. There were six such depots. The main one, which was located in Giesboro on the Potomac near Washington, was capable of handling 30,000 horses at one time. Situated on 625 acres, the depot encompassed stables, stockyards, storehouses, and quarters for hundreds of blacksmiths, carpenters, wagon makers, wheelwrights, farriers, and teamsters.

Seasoned troopers traveled light and lived off the land as much as possible. Pack animals and wagon trains carried the bulk of the supplies. On Union General James Wilson's expedition through Alabama with 12,000 horsemen, each trooper carried five days' worth of light rations, 100 rounds of ammunition, 24 pounds of grain, and two extra horseshoes. The 250 wagons and the pack animals in the supply train carried everything else.

The regulation U.S. army saddle was the McClellan, adopted on the recommendation of the man who devised it, General George B. McClellan, who apparently got the idea for the saddle on a tour of inspection in Europe just before the war. The saddle was an adaptation of the Mexican, or Texas, saddle, although it might have been fashioned after the Cossack saddle. It was light, strong, easy on the horse's back, and comfortable for the rider.

Union cavalrymen were armed with sabers, revolvers, and carbines. Initially, they carried the heavy 1860 dragoon saber, called the "Old Wristbreaker" by those who used it. It was replaced by the 1860 light cavalry saber, which had a 34-inch blade, a ridged grip, and a swept-back guard. The revolver generally carried was either a Colt percussion Army or Navy model or a Remington. A variety of carbines saw service in the Union cavalry. The most popular was the seven-shot Spencer, although the Sharps and the Burnside also were used.

The Confederate cavalryman also was armed with saber, revolver, and, when available, carbine. Confederate sabers were either Southern copies of Federal sabers or imports. The revolvers used were either captured Federal weapons or Southern copies of these weapons. Confederate cavalrymen usually carried two revolvers.

Units of irregulars carried the saber, but instead of the carbine, they might carry a rifle or a shotgun. The favorite weapon of Morgan's raiders was the two-band Enfield, a muzzle-loading import. The Sharps was well liked, and an armory in Richmond made copies.

As the Union cavalry improved, it placed more reliance on the saber. In some Confederate cavalry units, however, the saber was little used. The rifled musket, which penalized cavalry charges against entrenched infantrymen, brought a contempt for the saber. A Confederate general wrote that, when charged by Union cavalry, his men would cry: "Boys, here are those fools coming again with their sabers. Give it to them!"

In the partisan warfare in the West, the weapon of choice among the Confederate cavalry was the double-barreled shotgun. Riders would charge at full gallop, fire both barrels in their opponents' faces, then use their revolvers or pummel the enemy with the butts of their shotguns.

CORPS OF ENGINEERS

Before the war, the engineers of the U.S. Army were organized into two small but highly professional bodies—the Corps of Engineers and the Corps of Topographical Engineers. In 1863, these were merged and called the Corps of Engineers. As their name implies, the topographical engineers were principally mapmakers, but the duties of the two groups overlapped to such an extent that they can be considered as one unit from the start of the war.

The duties of the Corps of Engineers were many. The engineers were in charge of planning and superintending the construction of all fortifications and siege operations, as well as the construction and destruction of roads and bridges. The corps also had to furnish maps and detailed descriptions of terrain sufficient for planning troop movements. Engineers were attached to the various regimental staffs and reconnoitered the enemy's positions and chose routes and campsites.

The telegraph was one of many inventions that first saw military use in the Civil War. Here, a working crew of engineers are erecting poles and stringing wire. This was a constant task because the armies were often on the move, and Confederate cavalry took delight in unseating Union telegraph poles and cutting wire. (LC)

There was very little a Union engineer could not do. The small body of regular enlisted engineers was greatly expanded, and numerous volunteer engineer regiments were raised. These were officered either by regulars or by men with engineering training, of which the North had a good supply. In those days, Americans were familiar with the pick, the shovel, and the ax. The amount of work the engineers accomplished by manual labor was stupendous, and when necessary, they could fight as well as they could dig.

Few officers of the Confederate Corps of Engineers were experienced military engineers. Mostly they were men with technical training as civil engineers, some of whom had attended a military academy. These officers performed the same duties as their counterparts in the Union army—reconnaissance, mapmaking, fortifications, and the like. But until 1863, there was no provision for engineer troops in the Confederate army. Until then, engineering duties had been performed by the Pioneer Corps, which consisted of men detailed from the different divisions and directed by the engineers assigned to those divisions.

Both the Federal and Confederate armies were unable or, at times, unwilling to furnish sufficient men and equipment to their Corps of Engineers to complete important tasks. But in spite of these deficiencies, the engineers performed valuable and diverse services.

INFANTRY

An infantry regiment in the Union army at full strength consisted of 1,000 troops: 10 companies of 97 men and 3 officers each. Each company had 1 captain, 1 first lieutenant, 1 second lieutenant, 1 first sergeant, 4 sergeants, 8 corporals, 2 musicians, 1 wagoneer, and 81 privates. Commanding the regiment was a colonel assisted by another lieutenant colonel, a major, an adjutant (lieutenant), a quartermaster (lieutenant), a surgeon, and an assistant surgeon. In addition, there was 1 sergeant major, 1 regimental quartermaster sergeant, 1 hospital steward, 2 principal musicians, and 24 bandsmen (eliminated later in the war from most regiments and placed at corps headquarters).

A regiment, however, was seldom, if ever, at full strength. By the spring of 1863, regiments averaged 475 troops.

After the Battle of Fredericksburg, soldiers of the 6th Maine Infantry and their drummer boy stand at attention, bayonets fixed. Even in the heat of summer, soldiers wore the uniform blouses into battle. These men were participants in the attack across the stone wall at Marye's Heights, one of the bloodiest actions of the war, and were lucky to survive (NA)

The Union army usually allowed its volunteer regiments to dwindle away. When they were reduced to 150 to 200 men, they were broken up and new regiments were formed. This demoralizing system allowed state governors to appoint more colonels, a form of patronage that had an adverse effect on the management of the war.

The Confederate army tried to keep existing infantry regiments intact by feeding in recruits. As the war dragged on, though, many regiments were down to mere skeletons, but the esprit de corps continued. If the Union had adopted a similar system, using the existing regimental personnel as a cadre upon which to build, many disastrous defeats might have been avoided.

When possible, Confederate brigades were formed from regiments from one state. As a result, Southern troops had the same feeling of pride and loyalty toward their brigades as Northern soldiers had toward their regiments. Confederate units took the names of their original leaders, while a Union corps would be known by its number.

A Union regiment was known by its number and state—the 6th Vermont or the 11th Alabama, for example. Companies were designated by letters, starting with A, the senior captain's company, which held the post of honor on the right flank; then B, the next ranking company, on the left of the line; and so on.

Regiments usually were as good or as bad as their officers. Discipline and training by officers who knew their business, who took an interest in their men's health and welfare, and who "stood fire" well meant the difference between a regiment that "stayed put" and "took it" and a regiment that "skedaddled." Bravery among officers was of paramount importance, and a regiment without confidence in its officers was not likely to have confidence in itself.

During the war, there were attempts to create morale through the use of distinctive uniforms. A number of Zouave regiments were formed in the North and the South, complete with baggy pants, fezzes, and vivandieres. A famous Zouave drill team toured America before the war, and in emulation, the militia formed several Zouave companies. At the outbreak of the war, these were expanded into regiments.

Many of the fancy uniforms on both sides vanished during the first months of campaigning, though, and faded blue coats and light blue pants or home-dyed butternut uniforms became the standard.

In both the North and the South, infantry battle flags and regimental colors were carried into action by a color guard of handpicked noncommissioned officers. The colors acted as rallying points, were focal points for a regiment's strength and morale, and when seen from other points of the battlefield, acted as markers. Often, because of clouds of gun smoke, they were almost all that could be seen of the battle lines. However, the flags "drew lead like a magnet," and the brave color guards were frequently wiped out to a man. A regiment's "soul" was its colors, and it was better for a soldier to die than to lose the colors.

On the march, a brigade of four regiments of 600 men each would take up nearly 1,000 yards of road. With each man carrying 50 pounds or more of equipment, a regiment on good roads might cover 3 miles an hour, although heat and dust might slow this to two.

With baggage wagons, supply trains, artillery batteries, and ambulances accompanying the infantry brigade, competent staff work was essential. A regiment moving into the line of march at the wrong time could create a colossal traffic jam.

In battle, a regiment might fight with all its companies abreast, forming a long double line of men. Sometimes one or more companies would be held back as reserves or to guard the flanks. One or more companies usually were sent ahead to form a skirmish line. In a divisional attack, whole regiments might be used as skirmishers. Late in the war, skirmish lines grew heavier, sometimes consisting of half the regimental strength, the remainder being held in line of battle as a reserve. Skirmishers sought to keep down the enemy's fire and harass its ranks with musketry. Skirmish lines might be 400 or 500 yards in advance of the main formation.

As generals learned to their sorrow, bodies of men could not be moved with the ease and precision of chessmen. Many a charge that began with fixed bayonets, the rattle of drums, and fierce shouts lost momentum and ground to a halt at a respectable distance from the enemy.

During the first years of the war, the formations used were holdovers from the days when infantry weapons were not accurate beyond 100 yards. No attempt was made to modify existing tactics to keep pace with the development of the rifle. The resulting slaughter was as terrible as it was unnecessary.

Tents of many sizes and shapes were used during the war. Here, General George Meade stands before a tent without walls, which let a cool breeze through in the heat of summer. (LC)

The common sense of the veteran soldier came to the rescue. Instead of standing in ranks in the open, he learned to take cover whenever possible and to entrench wherever and however he could. If time and circumstance permitted, trees were felled, breastworks built, and trenches dug.

The veteran also learned to make a shrewd appraisal of the chances of success when ordered to attack fortified positions. On several occasions, veteran troops refused to advance in the face of certain death, leaving the assault to "green" regiments. If the veterans did advance, they were apt to do it in short rushes, lying down between volleys and taking advantage of such cover as the ground afforded. Willing to risk his life, the veteran soldier drew the line at throwing it away carelessly.

Realistic tactics evolved that conformed both to the terrain and to the new and deadly weapons with which the war was being fought. These tactics became standard practice in modern warfare, which reflects favorably on the intelligence and common sense of Civil War soldiers, Union and Confederate alike.

Experience also modified the soldier's equipment. The seasoned campaigner soon stripped down to the essentials, jettisoning anything superfluous. This was sometimes carried to extremes by inexperienced men, and coats and blankets discarded by hot, weary troops in the morning could be sorely missed at night.

In the Confederate Arm,y most equipment was in short supply, and although they also discarded all nonessentials, the lack of necessities was acute. But between the spinning wheels of their womenfolk and plunder from abundantly stocked Union supply depots, Confederate soldiers managed to keep going, and any deficiencies in their wardrobes were not reflected in their fighting ability.

At the beginning of the war, the need for firearms of any description was so great that many early types were purchased abroad and used by both sides until better weapons could be procured. This being the case, it is helpful to take a brief look at the developments leading up to the adoption of the rifled musket used by most infantry, Union and Confederate.

Before the invention of the Minie ball, rifles were issued only to a few special units because of the difficulty of loading. To grip the rifling properly, a ball had to be a tight fit and thus was harder to ram down after firing had clogged the bore. If the ball was made small enough to slip easily down a fouled barrel, it merely slid down the lands and did not bite into the grooves at all.

The U.S. army adopted the Minie bullet in 1852, rifling out some of the old .69-caliber smoothbore muskets. Many of these were used during the Civil War, and the peculiar whistle made by the Minie bullet became all too familiar to soldiers.

The Federal government did not arm its infantry with breechloaders. The ultraconservative Ordnance Department opposed anything new and also had a big investment in muskets. The effectiveness of breechloaders was beyond question, and the men wanted them so much that many companies purchased the guns themselves. It was a tragedy for the Union that the Ordnance Department hindered the adoption of the weapon that could have brought a speedy victory.

Few people firing offhand are capable of hitting a man-size target at more than 300 yards, even with a modern high-powered rifle, and the black-powder gun of the Civil War was anything but high-powered. Reaching a faraway target required using a high trajectory and estimating ranges carefully. Accuracy was further hampered when the air was full of whistling bullets, shell fragments, and gun smoke. It took a steady veteran to find his mark under those conditions. Many commanders preferred to hold their fire until the enemy was within 100 yards.

Volley firing also steadied the men. When loading "by the numbers," they were less likely to insert a cartridge bullet-first, to ram several charges one on top of the other (one musket picked up at Gettysburg had 23 loads in the barrel), or to make any of the many mistakes by which a nervous or excited man could disable his musket.

Some 37,000 muskets were salvaged after the Battle of Gettysburg. Of these, 24,000 were loaded, and of those, 18,000 had more than one load. And many of those with a single charge were loaded with untorn cartridges or with the bullet upside down.

By comparison, there were many instances when sharpshooters made remarkable hits at 700, 800, and even 1,000 yards, but they were experts firing from steady rests. Some were armed with heavy-barreled target rifles with telescopic sights, but the weight of such rifles precluded their use in ordinary combat.

Several unsuccessful attempts were made to interest the Union in machine guns with rotating multibarrels. The military opposed the idea, and few officers in authority expressed a need for a rapid-fire gun. General Ben Butler purchased a few machine guns, but they made no difference in his lackluster career. The Confederate Ordnance Department liked the idea, but couldn't manufacture the guns.

Three artillery sergeants strike a pose before a field tent. Although civilians associate swords with officers, noncommissioned officers of "Artillery, Cavalry, Infantry, and Foot Riflemen" were authorized to carry swords. Note that the artillery, like the cavalry, carried swords with curved blades. (NA)

Both North and South, the small arms used by officers and some enlisted men in the infantry were usually the standard five- or six-shot cap-and-ball revolvers of the period. Infantry officers and sergeants traditionally carried swords as emblems of rank, but they rarely used them as weapons.

The infantry of both sides used the bayonet. It was used as an entrenching tool, a can opener, a roasting spit, and for a number of other purposes, but it was seldom used as a weapon. Bayonets were fixed before a charge, but as Confederate General John Logan wrote of them: "The bristling points and the glitter of the bayonets were fearful to look upon as they were leveled in front of a charging line, but they were rarely reddened with blood."

Infantry reenactors unstack their rifles and break camp. Breech-loading, semiautomatic rifles were offered by manufacturers to the War Department. They were turned down because generals felt that such rifles would encourage soldiers to waste ammunition. (CT)

MEDICAL DEPARTMENT

More than 600,000 men died in the Civil War; of these nearly twice as many died of disease as were killed in battle. These are shocking figures, but too often the blame is laid solely on the medical profession. By and large, doctors did the best they could with imperfect knowledge, equipment, and techniques.

The Civil War was fought in a time when a stethoscope was a novelty, when there were fewer than 25 clinical thermometers in the entire Union army, and when such diseases as lockjaw, septicemia, malaria, and gangrene were believed to be caused by "evening dews and damps."

In a ward at the Carver General Hospital in Washington, D.C., soldiers, dressed in their uniform blouses, celebrate the Fourth of July. Although wartime medical care was primitive, the U.S. Sanitary Commission, organized by private citizens to help care for the wounded and sick, did a remarkable job of improving conditions. (LC)

Standards for personal hygiene and public health were all but nonexistent. The unsanitary and unhealthy conditions of normal civilian life of the period were multiplied by the gathering together in close quarters of huge numbers of men, many of whom looked on army life as an escape from the restrictions of society and did not wash their persons or their clothes very often.

Cold, damp, unsuitable, or inadequate clothing, atrocious food, and contaminated water all took their toll. Many recruits were young men from isolated areas, who were particularly susceptible to such common ailments as mumps, measles, and scarlet fever. Men unaccustomed to wet and exposure were subject to bad colds, which in turn often led to bronchitis and pneumonia. The scourge of all armies, dysentery, struck many, and communicable diseases of all kinds spread like wildfire.

If a Minie ball struck a soldier's arm or leg, it was a near certainty the limb would have to be amputated. The lead ball, larger than most modern bullets, expanded as it tore through flesh, mangling bones beyond repair. In the photograph, taken at Gettysburg, soldiers look on as a surgeon prepares to perform an amputation. (LC)

Recruits were barely examined physically, and the ranks included a high percentage of men with preservice disabilities such as epilepsy, syphilis, and the like.

Both sides made attempts to make conditions better, at least as far as hygiene and public health were concerned. Booklets on hygiene were distributed, and efforts were made to clean up the camps and provide proper latrines and toilet facilities.

The better the discipline of the unit, the better the men's health was likely to be. In regiments in which officers issued and enforced orders relating to sanitation, the sickness rate was much lower than in regiments in which the officers were too ignorant or too lazy to care.

As the war progressed, the troops became better able to take care of themselves. A veteran regiment in the field would show a far shorter sick list than a new regiment.

At first, a major problem was the collection and transportation of the wounded. There was no system and no central control. The collection was bad enough—men detailed for this task were usually the ones that the company commanders could best spare, the shirkers and the skulkers. Consequently, many wounded men were left unattended on the battlefield for days.

Many deaths and much suffering were a direct result of the medical service's failure to provide for moving the wounded from the regimental aid stations to the large general hospitals in the rear. Transportation of the wounded was handled by the Quartermaster Corps. The few ambulances were usually driven by civilians, who were apt to take off for the rear at the shriek of the first shell.

In 1862, General George B. McClellan issued an order setting up a much-improved system for the Army of the Potomac, which later became the standard for all Union armies. His system ensured, among other things, that ambulances and hospital supply wagons were no longer operated at the convenience of the Quartermaster Corps. Eventually, the Federal Ambulance Corps became a model organization.

The original system of regimental hospitals, which was basically the same in the North and the South, was cumbersome and inefficient. One regimental surgical staff might be overwhelmed by a rush of casualties, while another nearby might be inactive. In addition, some regimental surgeons seemed reluctant to treat the wounded of other regiments.

The Union wounded first walked or were carried to the forward dressing station, which the regimental medical officers established as close to the firing line as possible. After receiving first aid, they were loaded on ambulances and sent to the divisional field hospital, which was set up just out of artillery range. There the worst cases were operated on, and from there all who could be moved were sent to the base or general hospitals, of which, at one point, there were 205 Federal ones alone.

The average divisional hospital train consisted of 14 army wagons and 4 medical wagons, carrying 22 hospital tents as well as medical and surgical supplies and equipment sufficient to care for some 7,000 men.

The Confederate system was similar, except that most of the wounded were conveyed in ordinary wagons that were without springs and drawn by two mules. A few springed vehicles were used at first, but when they wore out, they could not be replaced. Transportation difficulties sometimes kept Confederate wounded in field hospitals for several weeks.

General hospitals on both sides grew in capacity and efficiency as the war progressed. Some were very large, even by modern standards. The great Chimborazo Hospital at Richmond, the largest military hospital in the world at the time, treated some 76,000 patients during the war. It could handle 4,800 patients in 150 one-story buildings, each 100 by 30 feet. Included on the 125-acre grounds were a bakery with a capacity of 10,000 loaves a day, an ice house, and soup kitchens, as well as a farm with 200 cows and a goat herd.

The Union's City Point Hospital was a merger of five corps hospitals. Partly under canvas, it had a huge capacity—6,000 to 10,000 patients in good weather. It even boasted a steam laundry.

Hospitals were generally well laid out and well ventilated. Fresh air was considered a must, partly because bad smells ("miasmas") were believed to cause or spread disease. Flies and mosquitoes were considered a nuisance and an irritation but were not suspected of spreading disease. Adequate plumbing was a rarity, and many seemingly modern hospital buildings had open latrines. On the plus side, disinfectants, deodorants, chlorine, and Dakin's solution (sodium hypochlorite) were widely used.

Both sides used railroad hospital trains, which might consist of specially fitted coaches used as kitchens, dispensaries, and surgeries or nothing more than a string of empty cattle cars well bedded with straw.

Surgery was more advanced than most realize. But a skillful surgeon might not know that his knife must be kept perfectly clean. The need to sterilize instruments was unknown. The surgeon wiped his knife on his dripping apron while waiting for the next patient, and the nurse or an aid rinsed out the bloodstained sponges in the same filthy water that had stood by the operating table all day.

Amputations were frequent because of the terrible wounds caused by the heavy bullets fired from rifled muskets, and many were performed in the most primitive surroundings, often on a kitchen table in an open shed by surgeons half dead from overwork.

Wounds were supposed to suppurate ("laudable pus" was the term used), and that they could heal without inflammation was unthinkable. Maggots were sometimes used to clean wounds. Water dressings were used for large wounds and amputations.

Chloroform was the only available anesthetic, and morphine and opium were used to relieve pain. Despite reports to the contrary, many Confederate surgeons were adequately supplied with chloroform and morphine.

At the start of the war, the U.S. Army Medical Department numbered 115; 24 resigned and went South to become the nucleus of the Medical Department of the Confederacy. A number of surgeons entered the service with the formation of the Union's volunteer regiments. Many were country doctors of varying degrees of proficiency, and others were simply quacks. Examination boards looked the other way when the demand for surgeons far outran the supply.

There were some female nurses, usually assigned to the general hospitals. They had to contend with the outspoken antagonism of high-ranking medical men who resented their incursion into a man's domain. Their work was universally appreciated by their patients, who got only scant attention from the enlisted men and convalescents who made up most of the nursing staff.

Numerous relief agencies attempted to do for the soldiers what the government could not or would not do. The most powerful of these was the U.S. Sanitary Commission. It represented many influential people and wielded considerable power in Washington. During the war, the commission distributed some $15 million worth of supplies. Its work was supported by contributions and money raised by various clubs and social groups.

Besides inspecting camps, their locations, drainage, and food and recommending improvements, the Sanitary Commission distributed food, clothing, and medical supplies. Later in the war, the increased efficiency of the Medical Department made some of the commission's work supplementary, but until the end, a Sanitary Commission wagon was with every corps, dispensing such essentials as chloroform, bandages, beef stock, chewing tobacco, and writing paper.

The commission also ran hospital ships that transported thousands of wounded, while its "homes" fed and sheltered soldiers on leave, recruits on their way to their regiments, and men recently discharged.

NAVY

When war came, the Union had a small, outdated, undermanned navy, and the Confederacy had no navy at all. With no opposition, the Union navy was able to blockade Confederate seaports, destroy coastal forts, and take control of inland water highways from the outset. As the war progressed, the Confederacy did form its own navy, but because of its inferior manufacturing capability, it was never able to close the gap entirely.

No branch of the Federal government was more poorly prepared for war than the navy. This led to the surrender of Fort Sumter, the loss of Pensacola, and the disaster at the Norfolk Navy Yard, where 10 warships were burned, the navy yard and its buildings and stores were destroyed, and hundreds of cannons were abandoned to the enemy. To make matters worse, one out of five navy officers defected to the Confederacy.

The officers of the USS Kearsage *have good reason to be proud as they pose for the photographer. The steamer fought and sank the famed Confederate raider* Alabama *in a duel off the harbor at Cherbourg, France, on April 8, 1863. Fifteen members of the crew received Medals of Honor for gallantry in the action. (NA)*

When Gideon Welles, Lincoln's secretary of the navy, was ordered to blockade more then 3,500 miles of Southern coast in 1861, the navy's ships were
scattered all over the globe. The blockade also turned out to be a diplomatic
mistake. Under international law, nations only "blockade" the ports of enemy
nations. When Lincoln proclaimed the blockade, it constituted the recognition of the Confederacy as a nation.

To acquire more ships, U.S. navy officials went throughout the Northern
ports to buy or charter "everything afloat that could be made of service." The
Navy Department itself began building 8 sloops of war, and private yards
were contracted to build 23 gunboats. Before Welles was through, more than
500 armed ships would fly the Stars and Stripes.

Manning the new ships was a problem. At the start of the war, there were
fewer than 8,000 naval personnel. By the end, there were more than 50,000,
most of whom had never been aboard a ship before joining the navy. A high
percentage of ordinary seamen in the Union navy were immigrants who did
not mind the rough life and low pay. Blacks were allowed in the navy as early
as late 1861.

Even more serious, however, was the shortage of trained officers. The
three upper classes at the U. S. Naval Academy were put on active duty, but
this was only a beginning. Many more officers came from the Union's large
merchant fleet.

In the prewar Union, navy officers were promoted by seniority, and there
was no provision for retiring older officers. This filled the higher grades with
elderly men who were neither innovative nor enterprising. Many admirals
were unfit for command, and the officers under them had no command
experience. To help combat this problem, fitness reviews and a law requiring
retirement at age 62 were instituted early in the war.

Warships were usually crowded, and the diet of the seamen was poor and
monotonous, usually consisting of salted meat and hardtack, which did little
for health or morale. Fresh meat and vegetables were seldom available, and
then only in quantities barely sufficient to ward off scurvy. At first, sailors age
21 and older were eligible for a daily half-pint of wine or quarter-pint of rum.
But in 1862, even this small comfort was denied when Congress ruled that

A gun crew unlimbers a Dahlgren gun aboard a U.S. warship. The gun was invented by Admiral John A. Dahlgren, who commanded the Washington Navy Yard when war broke out. There were three types: bronze 12- and 14-pounders for use on riverboats, iron smoothbore shell guns, and iron rifles, all the best of their kind. (LC)

"the spirit ration in the Navy of the United States shall forever cease."

The Union navy devoted most of its attention to the work of strangling the South by blockade. Because of the great extent of coastline to be watched, the fleet was divided into squadrons and still smaller flotillas.

The North American Squadron patrolled the coast of Virginia and North Carolina; the South Atlantic Squadron, from there south to Florida. The East Gulf Squadron patrolled southern and western Florida; the West Gulf Squadron, from Pensacola to the Rio Grande. The Mississippi Squadron fought to take and hold that vast and vital river system, while the small Pacific Squadron kept watch in the West. The Potomac Flotilla patrolled that river, often in ships and cutters, while being sniped at from the banks and frequently running aground on the many flats and shoals.

Other ships were on detached duty in pursuit of Confederate privateers and cruisers and on routine foreign service. The crews of these were handpicked and probably contained a higher percentage of veteran sailors.

Most Northern ironclads were of the type that received its name from the first of its kind, the *Monitor*. This class of vessel carried its armament in one or more revolving armored towers mounted on a hull with very little freeboard. An armored pilothouse was usually mounted on top of one of the turrets but did not revolve with it. The deck was also armored. Smokestacks, partially armored, as well as davits, ventilators, and the like were the only projections on the deck.

Armor consisted of wrought iron bolted onto heavy wooden backing. Turret armor on Federal ships was usually about 8 inches thick. This was impervious to shell, usually shattering cast-iron shot, but it could be penetrated by large-caliber shot of wrought iron fired with battering charges.

The monitors were quite seaworthy, although with their exceptionally low freeboard, they could not fight in heavy seas. And while the monitors were nearly invulnerable, their offensive power was quite limited, primarily because they were slow moving. They also had a slow rate of fire because the loading space for the gun crew was small and the guns were large.

River gunboats were in a class by themselves. Strictly shoal-water boats, they were almost exclusively side- or stern-wheelers. Screws at the time were not well adapted for shallow water, and they tended to lose power and were easily damaged. Some river gunboats were specially designed and built for use in the war; others were existing craft, armed and sometimes armored. Union gunboats built by Eads carried only light armor, and that did not cover the whole casemate.

Not only did the Confederacy start the war without ships, but no manu-facturer in the South was capable of building marine engines sufficiently powerful for a warship. Iron was scarce, as were the mills to roll it into plates. The navy yard at Norfolk was a wreck, while the only other, at Pensacola, was equipped solely for repair work.

Yet the Confederate Navy Department, under the resourceful Stephen R. Mallory, performed miracles of improvisation. It scoured the countryside for scrap iron and ripped up railway road tracks for armor, and by war's end, it had built 37 ironclads of varying types. It also purchased any ships in the South that could serve a useful purpose in the war, as well as vessels from abroad. It even established a naval academy, complete with training ship.

Recruits were plentiful, but few of them were seamen. The crews of most of the ships built abroad consisted largely of foreigners, mostly British, though the officers were Southerners.

The first Confederate armored ram, the CSS *Virginia,* was built on the hull and engines of the USS *Merrimack,* which was in the Norfolk navy yard when the yard was seized. Other Confederate ironclads usually followed the pattern of the *Merrimack*—a sloping-sided armored structure pierced for guns that were carried on the hull, whose bow and stern projected some distance beyond the casemate and which either had a very low freeboard or was submerged completely.

The Confederates' river gunboats were subject to the same problems as the Union's, with many of the steamers and rams protected only with wood and bales of cotton.

When war came, the Union had a small, antiquated navy, and the Confederacy had no navy at all. Both sides purchased civilian boats and ships to help meet the need. Shown in the photograph is the CSS Commander Perry, *a prewar ferry. Forced to innovate, the Confederate navy came up with the ironclad and a workable submarine. (LC)*

Most Confederate vessels were underpowered and suffered from defective engines. Northern engineering was far superior, but none of the ironclads of either navy were capable of any great speed. Six knots was about average for the monitors, and the river ironclads could not do much better.

Searching for some way to counter the superior Union naval forces, the Confederates developed a new type of warship. It was a small, iron, steam-driven, cigar-shaped vessel that was submersible—that is, it could take on sufficient water ballast to submerge most of its hull, leaving only a small amount of deck, conning tower, and smokestack showing. These "Davids" carried spar torpedoes.

A true, if crude, submarine, the *Hunley* (which earned the nickname "Peripatetic Coffin" by drowning three crews and its inventor, Horace L. Hunley) managed to bring her spar torpedo in contact with one large Union ship, the *Housatonic*. The resulting explosion sent both vessels to the bottom.

Naval weapons were as varied as the ships themselves. The standard broadside gun in the Federal navy was the 9-inch Dahlgren. It was supplemented by heavier guns mounted on pivots that could be brought to bear on either beam and that, if located on poop or forecastle, gave a wide arc of fire. Smaller vessels often carried 6.4-inch 32-pounders as broadside guns. The *New Ironsides,* on the other hand, mounted 11-inch guns on the broadside. The heaviest gun in use was the 15-inch, which was mounted in some of the monitors. The smallest was the 12-pounder howitzer.

The Union used many rifled guns—mostly Parrots, ranging from the 20-pounder up to the 8-inch 150-pounder. The Confederates used many Brooke rifles. These generally were heavier than the Parrots of corresponding caliber because, while the Parrot had only one reinforcing hoop at the breech, the Brooke had several. The Confederates also used assorted British imports, but a great deal of their armament was U.S. naval material seized at Norfolk or other yards at the beginning of the war.

For close work, both sides used grapeshot and canister. Canister was effective up to 300 yards; grapeshot, up to 400 yards or even up to 1,000 yards against personnel and small boats. Both were used in running past forts and earthworks to drive enemy gunners from their embrasures.

One of the innovations of the war was the mine, like this Confederate barrel mine. Mines were often called torpedoes, and it was the mines in Mobile Bay that Admiral Farragut referred to when he ordered, "Damn the torpedoes! Full speed ahead!" (NA)

Mines were the natural defensive weapons for a weaker naval power, and the Confederates employed mines of great variety and ingenuity. But the mine fields may have been even more effective at undermining enemy morale than they were at causing physical damage. Four monitors and 3 ironclad gunboats were among some 27 Union vessels sunk by mines.

The torpedo used in submersibles consisted of a container of explosive mounted on the end of a spur, rigged so that it could be carried out of the water and lowered when the attack was about to be made. These torpedoes were detonated by contact, and the boats used to carry them were usually steam launchers.

In addition to its navy, the Confederacy made good use of privateers. (Privateering is the arming and manning of a vessel by private persons holding a commission from the government to operate against an enemy, usually his merchantmen.) A wide variety of ships were used for privateering—armed boats, an ironclad (the *Manassas),* schooners, steamers, and submarines. Most were small, carried few guns, and accomplished little.

The big raiders were another matter. They were all well armed and officered by Confederate naval men. Most, like the *Florida,* the *Alabama,* and the *Georgia,* were British-built. The *Nashville* was a Northern ship seized in a Southern port at the outbreak of war. While having little or no effect on the outcome of the war, these cruisers did great damage to American commerce, damage from which it took years to recover. In all, they took 261 vessels, most of which they destroyed.

The Confederacy also had the help of blockade-runners. Many picked up supplies in the neutral ports of Bermuda or Nassau and made the run to Savannah or Wilmington. When entering a Confederate port, a runner usually carried a potpourri of essentials and luxuries—bonnet frames, boots, brandy, quinine, rifles, saddles, saltpeter, sherry, and tea. Outward-bound, it was piled high with cotton.

Many blockade-runners were British-built and British-owned. At one time, half the shipyards in England were building vessels for running the blockade, and some of these vessels were commanded by officers on extended leave from the Royal Navy.

The task of the blockade-runner—to get into a Southern port with much-needed supplies and out again with a hold full of cotton—was risky but profitable. The price of cotton was also soaring. Bales that could be bought for 6 cents a pound in the South were fetching 56 to 66 cents a pound in England. The profit on a single bale was at least $50. A vessel might well pay for herself in one successful round trip.

Wages paid to blockade-runners were also high. When the trade was at its peak, a successful captain might expect $5,000 for a run to a Southern port and back, and even deck hands earned $250 a trip.

Blockade-runners relied on their speed, their knowledge of the waters, and their invisibility at night. Runners painted their ships dull gray, and some even lowered their ships' boats to the rail to further minimize their silhouettes. With proper caution, a runner could slip undetected by a blockader at 200 yards.

QUARTERMASTER CORPS

The duties and responsibilities of the Federal Quartermaster Corps were many and difficult. This corps was charged with supplying and clothing the troops, providing shelter for them in the form of barracks or tents, and transporting them by land or water. It furnished vehicles and the horses and mules to draw them, found mounts for the cavalry, and built docks, ships, roads, and bridges. It built and purchased wagons by the tens of thousands, and its huge wagon trains could be found on almost every road in the war zone. Its repair shops alone employed thousands. During the war, the Federal government appropriated more than $1 billion to the Quartermaster Corps.

The Confederate Quartermaster Corps served the same function as its Federal counterpart, but with one major difference: It had only a fraction of the supplies to distribute. With little manufacture of its own, the Confederacy relied primarily on imports run through the blockade. In its favor, the

The engine President *chugs into the depot of the U.S. Military Railroad at City Point during the siege of Petersburg. Henry Haupt, Grant's chief of railroads, cut through red tape to get his job done. Union troops wanted for nothing as they pounded Lee's starving men. At the end, it was a war of manpower and supplies. (LC)*

Confederacy was fighting on its own soil and did not need vast and vulnerable wagon trains like those that followed the invading Federal columns.

At the beginning of the war, the Confederates were able to equip themselves to a degree from captured Federal supplies. Bad leadership that led to several disastrous defeats and poorly guarded trains and supply depots enabled rebel troops to help themselves to Federal supplies on many occasions. But such opportunities grew scarcer and scarcer as the war went on, and the Confederates simply had to tighten their belts and fight on.

In contrast, Federal soldiers fared better as the war progressed. Better supervision over purchasing of supplies meant better materials. More efficient distribution meant fewer shortages. Today's American soldier would have found the conditions under which his Civil War counterpart fought intolerable—his clothing unsuitable, his boots and equipment uncomfortable, and his food inedible. Yet never before in history had any army been so well equipped, nor had so much been done for its comfort and well-being.

The field organization of the Federal Quartermaster Corps called for a quartermaster for each regiment (a lieutenant), a quartermaster for each brigade (a captain), and a quartermaster for each division (a major). A lieutenant colonel was chief quartermaster of each army corps, and a colonel was chief quartermaster of an army. All of these had their assistants and staffs. At every level, the work was demanding, the responsibility heavy, and the rewards few.

The wagon trains were enormous. Twenty-five wagons per thousand men was the usual ratio. McClellan's trains in the Peninsula campaign contained some thousand wagons, as did General William T. Sherman's during the Atlanta campaign. All of these wagon trains had to be carefully routed, and the traffic problems and timetables were usually complicated and difficult.

On both sides, a large proportion of transports were used in the feeding of troops. It was a gargantuan task to feed the hundreds of thousands of hungry men, many of them far away from supply bases. Sometimes the men themselves carried rations for 5 to 10 days, but eventually the wagons had to get through, and the state of the roads was as important as the location of enemy troops. Rain and thaw often made movement all but impossible.

Not all food was transported by wagon. "Beef on the hoof" followed most armies. Though often underfed and overdriven, these beefs were a welcome change from raw pork and hardtack infested with weevils.

Commissary stores were obtained through contracts and then apportioned to the armies, the corps, the divisions, the brigades, and finally, the regiments, which distributed the rations to the troops.

Early in the war, the Confederacy found that meat and grain were scarce and ordered grain crops to be planted instead of cotton. This made more food available, but not always where it was most needed.

Some canned goods were available, but they were expensive luxuries. There were attempts to use "desiccated" vegetables—vegetables that had been scalded, dried, and pressed into cakes—but these were universally disliked by soldiers.

The daily allowance for the Federal soldier in camp was ¾ pound of fresh beef or 1¼ pounds of salted beef; 1 pound of hardtack; less than ⅓ cup of dried peas or beans; less than ¼ cup of rice or hominy; 1¼ ounces of ground and roasted coffee or enough tea to make 3 cups; ¼ cup of sugar; a little vinegar; about 1 tablespoon of salt; a pinch of pepper; a swallow of molasses; and occasionally, ¼ pound of potatoes. Together, this food amounted to about 2,300 calories, but it was very low in vitamins. And often, the soldier got much less.

Federal rations were occasionally augmented by dried fruits, fresh vegetables, and pickled cabbage to prevent malnutrition and disease. The Sanitary Commission and various state organizations tried to fill the gap by shipping barrels of potatoes, onions, and apples.

The Confederate ration certainly *was* less than the Federal—and more likely to be cut. At the beginning of the Gettysburg campaign, the daily ration for General Lee's troops was ½ pound of bacon, 1 pound of flour, ¼ cup of peas, less than 1 ounce of sugar, and a little salt.

Coffee was drunk in large quantities—with meals, between meals, and at every halt long enough to start a small fire. Though condensed milk was sometimes available (Gail Borden had patented the process in 1856), coffee was usually drunk black and scalding hot.

In camp or winter quarters, cooks chosen through a rotation process did the cooking. They often were men who were too lazy and dirty to make presentable soldiers, and often the quality of the cooking was worse than the quality of the food. Thus, many men chose to cook for themselves.

The Federal marching ration was 1 pound of hardtack, ¾ pound of salt pork or 1¼ pounds of fresh pork, coffee, sugar, and salt. Soldiers carried their rations in their haversacks and cooked their own meat and coffee over the campfire. If fires couldn't be lit, they ate the pork raw. A favorite sandwich was slices of raw pork, sprinkled with brown sugar, between two pieces of hardtack. Soups and stews were popular, as practically anything edible could be used in them. Worms were often found in the hardtack. One soldier wrote of finding 37 worms in one cracker, but, he said, "we eat them without looking."

Union soldiers pose before a log hut that served as a company kitchen at a winter encampment somewhere in Virginia. While campaigning, troops usually carried rations of hard tack and preserved beef and cooked for themselves. Though not appetizing, these rations would seem almost a veritable banquet to Confederate soldiers. (LC)

When marching rations were gone, the troops foraged. In friendly territory, this took the form of going house to house begging for handouts or confiscating a few apples and ears of corn and perhaps a stray chicken. In

A thirsty reenactor is served lemonade at the Christian Commission tent. Besides providing food and nursing care, the commission ran libraries stocked with Bibles and newspapers in army camps, and provided paper and pens so that soldiers could write home. (CT)

enemy territory, the local inhabitants could expect to have their larders stripped clean.

The sutler was the other source of supply for the Federal soldier. A sutler was a civilian, a sort of mobile Post Exchange, and one was allowed for each regiment. Sutlers were appointed either by the governor of the regiment's home state or by the regimental officers.

Among the articles found on a sutler's shelves were candy, canned goods, cheese, fish, fruit, loaf sugar, soft drinks (a sutler who sold whiskey could lose his license), books, clothing, cutlery, paper, paper collars, and razors.

Although prices were set by the army, many sutlers made outrageous profiteering on their virtual monopoly. To make matters worse, the sutler could attach the pay of any man, officer or enlisted, who owed him money.

Some men dispensed their own justice to a gouging sutler by raiding his establishment. A tent rope might be cut or the wagon overturned. Then the troops would swoop down, help themselves to the sutler's wares, and run away. Usually, if the sutler was reasonably honest and tried to get along with the troops, he had little to fear. He could argue that he had to charge high prices to make up for the risks he ran in the field.

SIGNAL CORPS

The very nature of the Civil War necessitated the development of the Signal Corps. Never before on this continent had such great armies marched and fought over such a vast area. It soon became apparent that both the Union and the Confederacy needed a comprehensive system of long-distance communications.

The Confederates acted first, organizing a corps of signalers in 1861 under the command of General E. P. Alexander, who later became chief of artillery. This corps was attached to the Adjutant General's Department and handled signaling, telegraphy, and secret-service work.

At the outbreak of the war, the Union's signal unit consisted only of Major A. J. Meyer, the inventor of the army's signal system. Eventually, the unit grew to some 300 officers and 2,500 enlisted men, formed under Meyer's command. At first, this unit suffered severely from departmental jealousies, and it was not until the summer of 1864 that it was organized as a separate Signal Corps.

Signaling on both sides was accomplished with flags, torches, lights, rockets, and flares. On the battlefield, signal guns were used to ensure concerted action in a prearranged attack. High points of land, if available, or wooden towers were used as vantage points. Chains of such points relayed messages with rapidity and accuracy, although occasionally they were interrupted by rain, fog, or snow.

The signal service was dangerous. A group of signalers near the battlefield was a favorite target for rifle or artillery fire. Signalmen on their exposed perches were regularly picked off by snipers.

Signalers sent messages by waving a signal flag, torch, or light from up to the right to the left and back (one) or down to the right and up (two). Combinations of these numbers stood for letters, phrases, and numerals. The flags used were either white with a red square in the middle or red with a white square, depending on the weather conditions and the time of day. Colored lights or rockets were used in combinations for prearranged sets of signals.

The signalers were enlisted men, sending the numbers read off by the officer in charge. A constant station-to-station watch was kept by men with powerful telescopes, on the alert to receive a message at any hour of the day or night.

Navy signals were different from those used on land, so if cooperation between the two services was required, army signal officers were carried aboard ship. This was particularly useful in directing naval gunfire at shore targets.

Besides the mechanical means employed by the Signal Corps of both armies, there was much use of the whip and spur, as well-mounted couriers sped between nearby headquarters.

Messages were seldom sent in "clear," because wigwag flags and swinging torches might be seen by the enemy. Ciphers and codes of various types and complexities were employed. One quick way to encipher a message was to use a cipher disk, which matched letters of the alphabet with signal numbers.

In cipher, every letter of the "clear" message stands for another letter, a symbol, or an entire message. In code, a code word represents a phrase, a sentence, or an entire message. Codes are limited in scope and can only be employed with a code book. But any message, however complicated, can be sent in cipher, and the receiver only has to know the key to be able to decipher it; no code books or code dictionaries are necessary.

During the Civil War, cryptographers on both sides worked hard to interpret the messages sent by their opponents, which meant that ciphers and codes were constantly being changed. In this activity, the North was more successful than the South. Although the Confederates used a relatively complicated system, the Federal experts had no difficulty breaking down Confederate communications. And while the Federals used a simple word-transposition cipher, the Confederates never broke down a single Federal message.

Both armies depended heavily on the telegraph, yet both relied on poorly paid civilian railroad personnel to operate their telegraph systems. In the Confederate army, the railroads were under the control of the Signal Corps. In the Federal army, they operated as part of a successful bureau, the U.S. Military-Telegraph Corps, which was attached to the Quartermaster Corps.

The Federal telegraph system was rigidly controlled by the War Department. The officers who supervised the system reported only to the secretary of war. Even the telegraph operators in the various theaters were completely independent of the commanding generals.

The Federal government took over the telegraph lines around Washington, D.C., in 1861 and the remainder the following year. The South relied on the cooperation of the private telegraph companies for the use of lines.

On both sides, the field telegraph, when possible, linked the headquarters of the armies in the field with the capital and with the headquarters of the corps commanders. Construction crews kept the main line up with the army when it advanced, running loops to corps headquarters. Cable was strung on short poles or on trees.

Thousands of miles of field cable were strung, often under enemy fire. During the last year of the war, more than 1,750,000 messages were transmitted over the Federal telegraph system alone.

An interesting adjunct to the Federal and Confederate Signal Corps was the military balloon.

Throughout history, generals have wanted to know what was going on over the hill, so it was not surprising that when men first ascended in a balloon, the military establishment immediately saw it as a potential tool. Balloons were used during the French Revolution, but they accomplished little beyond shaking enemy morale. The problem was, it was one thing to see what was happening, and quite another to interpret what was seen in terms of strategy and tactics.

In the 1850s, ballooning became widely known. Aeronauts gave exhibition flights at county fairs and were publicized in the press. Several of these aeronauts offered their services to the Federal government during the Civil War and served on various fronts. The sight of huge gas bags rising slowly, often drawing enemy fire, became familiar to ground troops.

Thaddeus Lowe, a celebrated balloonist, organized a Balloon Corps for the Union. From July 1861 to March 1862, the corps under Lowe operated two balloons for the Army of the Potomac, ascending above the lines to observe enemy camps. Often, the observers could estimate almost down to a platoon the size of the rebel forces by the number of camp fires. From their

One technological innovation used by the Union army was the observation balloon, such as this one being inflated during the Battle of Fair Oaks, Virginia, in 1862. Balloons helped track troop movements and the accuracy of artillery fire. Other innovations included repeating rifles, rifled cannons, exploding shells, and ironclad warships. (NA)

balloons, the observers transmitted information to the ground, using light telegraph wire. They also made sketches while aloft and observed the Confederate lines around Richmond through telescopes.

By early 1862, Lowe had seven balloons in operation. Lowe used the telegraph in the first aerial direction of artillery fire in history. But the full potential of the Balloon Corps was never realized.

Aeronauts of the Balloon Corps enjoyed a quasimilitary status, which rankled their military superiors. In particular, the chief engineer disliked that Lowe had so much freedom and that he sometimes circumvented army channels to obtain needed supplies.

During the movement north to intercept General Lee's invasion of Pennsylvania, General Hooker ordered the Signal Corps to take over the Balloon Corps. When the Signal Corps commander protested that he did not have sufficient manpower or funds to do so, the balloon train was ordered back to Washington and disbanded.

Thus, the Union army lost a valuable tool. As it was, the Confederates went to considerable lengths to conceal their movements whenever a Northern balloon was in evidence. Alexander, head of the Confederate Signal Corps, remarked that the Balloon Corps would have been worth keeping for its nuisance value alone.

Not much is known about Confederate balloon activity, although there was mention in the Northern press of a Confederate observation balloon being used at Falls Church, Virginia, in June 1861. On August 22, 1861, General Joseph Johnston wrote to General P. T. G. Beauregard that "it seems to me that the balloon may be useful . . . . Let us send for it; we can surely use it advantageously."

General James Longstreet wrote that, in early 1862, the Confederates gathered silk dresses and made a balloon—"a great patchwork ship of many varied hues which was ready for use in the Seven Days' campaign. The meanest trick of the war and one that I have never yet forgiven."

Both sides attempted to shoot down enemy balloons, but the inability to elevate their cannons sufficiently high, combined with tricky artillery fuses, frustrated their efforts. To avoid being fired on by their own troops, Union aeronauts marked their balloons with red, white, and blue bunting. One balloon, nicknamed the "Constitution," was decorated with a large portrait of George Washington. Another, the "Union," had a gigantic spread eagle and the Stars and Stripes.

This Virginia state seal flag, now in the collection of the Museum of the Confederacy in Richmond, was carried into battle by Virginia troops. The Old Dominion took its first vote to secede on April 17, 1861, and its flag was adopted three days later. The seal, which dates from the Revolution, fetters the figure of "Liberty" and the Latin inscription Sic Semper Tyrannis (Ever Thus to Tyrants). Virginia's troops were called to the colors the same day that the convention voted on secession. (MOC)

ANTIQUES & COLLECTIBLES

A

ACCOUTERMENTS, CONFEDERATE. In the Civil War, the term *accouterments* applied only to a soldier's belt and the items worn on his belt or over his shoulder. These included the cartridge box, the cap box, and the bayonet scabbard. The canteen, the haversack, and the knapsack usually were not considered accouterments. The accouterments of most interest to the collector are the cartridge box and the cap box.

Due to shortages of materials, the Confederacy either imported its accouterments from England or improvised substitute materials. Layers of cotton cloth, for instance, were stitched together in three or four thicknesses to be used in place of leather. Lead and wood replaced brass for fittings.

Quantities of cartridge boxes were imported from England as part of the equipment used with Enfield rifles. Boxes manufactured in the Confederacy had the same proportions as the U.S. issue, but the leather was of poorer

Personal possessions and memorabilia of General J. E. B. Stuart, Lee's cavalry commander, are displayed at the Museum of the Confederacy in Richmond. At the upper left is his headquarters flag on which rest Stuart's field glasses and case and haversack. Below are Stuart's jacket, wool vest and trousers, his frock coat and plumed felt officer's hat, a Calisher and Terry carbine and leather gun case, and another pair of field glasses. The revolver on the left is a Whitney carried by Stuart at Yellow Tavern, where he was mortally wounded; on the right side is the LeMat revolver and holster he carried through much of the war. Below is a Model 1860 cavalry saber and a captured Federal officer's sword belt and plate. Above are his cavalry boots and his McClellan saddle. On the saddle are his buckskin gauntlets and a silk sash. A tin cup, wash basin, and bowl complete the array. (MOC)

quality and very rough on the inside. The outside was smooth black leather, occasionally impressed with a "C.S." in an oval cartouche.

Confederate cap boxes are very rare, particularly if they have the impressed "C.S." within an oval. Forged Confederate cap boxes have turned up on the market, but they are easily distinguishable to the trained eye.

ACCOUTERMENTS, FEDERAL. Federal accouterments included only the soldier's belt and items worn on the belt or over the shoulder. Accouterments varied for the three main branches of the army—artillery, cavalry, and infantry.

Artillerymen could carry a sword in a scabbard and a pistol in a holster. One gunner wore the gunner's belt and fuse pouch.

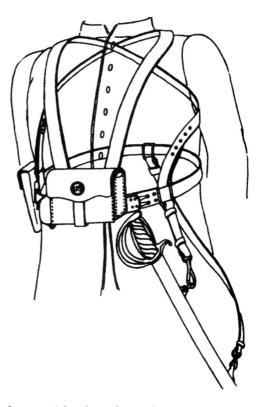

Mann's accouterments, designed to re-place unsatisfactory early cavalry accouterments, were introduced late in the war. By placing the weight on the shoulders, they were more comfortable than earlier models. (NA)

Cavalry accouterments included a cartridge box for carbine ammunition, a pistol box for revolver ammunition, and a cap box. The saber in its scabbard and the revolver in its holster were not considered accouterments, although they were attached to the belt. The carbine was attached to the carbine sling and worn over the shoulder.

Infantry accouterments consisted of a cartridge-box sling, a cartridge box, a cap box, and a bayonet scabbard.

The waist belt of enlisted men was of black leather fastened by a belt buckle. The belt buckle was a brass oval with "U.S." in large black letters in the middle or, alternatively, letters designating the regiment's home state. Noncommissioned officers wore a belt similar to commissioned officers, but it had a rectangular belt buckle with an American eagle or the state coat of arms.

Cartridge boxes were made of leather. On the side of the cartridge box was a plate similar in appearance to the buckle on the enlisted man's belt.

The plate was a brass oval shield stamped with the letters "U.S." or with letters or insignia designating the regiment's state. Both cartridge-box plates and belt buckles have been reproduced in vast quantities, and collectors should investigate carefully to make sure they aren't paying inflated prices for reproductions.

The infantry experimented with many types of cartridge boxes. The Bennett cartridge box used springs to open the cover automatically. The Bush cartridge box employed sliding metallic boxes within the leather cartridge box. The Domis cartridge box had a cylindrical revolving case with chambers to hold cartridges. The Hirschbuhl cartridge box contained compartments to hold the different articles of ammunition, including a compartment for a powder box; attached to one side were separate boxes holding bullets, percussion caps, and balls. The Pease cartridge box had compartments opening at the side to hold bullet patches, swabs, and an oil bottle, with a cap pouch in the front of the box. The Smith cartridge box contained vertical tubes to receive two cartridges, one on top of the other. The Warren cartridge box contained two tin compartments; when the upper one was empty, the other could be rotated into position without detaching it from the leather box. The Warren and Chesebrough cartridge box held both cartridges and caps in a circular

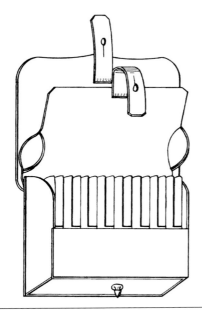

Smith's cartridge box, the brainchild of a Brooklyn, New York, inventor, allowed two cartridges, one above the other, to be stored in its vertical tubes. (NA)

revolving box in a circular case. The Weston cartridge box had a series of spring-operated blades that cut the paper ends of the cartridge rows. The Wilson cartridge box had a spring fastening to hold the box open or closed.

The cap box, containing percussion caps, was of black leather. The infantry used four types of cap boxes: the Harvey cap box, which consisted of a ring-shaped cap holder within a cylindrical case; the Lamb cap box, which had notched revolving plates joined at their centers; the Pickett percussion cap holder, which allowed the caps to be arranged in a row on a belt in an oblong box; and the Warren cap box, which used a spring to eject the cap into a cup-shaped mouth, where it could be grasped easily.

Union troops carried two bayonet scabbards: the leather Gaylord bayonet scabbard and later the steel Emerson bayonet scabbard.

AIGUILLETTES. The aiguillette was an ornamental cord worn on the uniform. Some Federal staff officers and adjutants wore aiguillettes with a gold cord. Light artillerymen in the Union army wore a red aiguillette when wearing the Model 1864 light artillery shako.

AMMUNITION, SMALL-ARMS. Ammunition was more varied than the weapons themselves. Neither North nor South had a central arsenal for fabricating small-arms ammunition, and even with strict guidelines, the 16 Federal arsenals and the 18 smaller Confederate arsenals often made different cartridges and bullets for the same weapons. This situation was further complicated by the purchase of arms from private manufacturers at home and abroad.

Weapon inventors and manufacturers made rifles and pistols that required their patented cartridges, which forced authorities to purchase ammunition from them. Private manufacturers also were constantly trying to interest the government in new bullets and cartridges. Some were worthless, but others had merit and were put into production.

Small-arms ammunition, North and South, ranged from simple to complex. Although it was possible to load most weapons with loose powder and ball, this was against regulations and therefore was not done.

Muzzleloaders commonly used paper-wrapped cartridges. The bullet and powder charge were encased in paper, often requiring soldiers to open the round to pour the powder down the barrel. The paper had to be removed on Federal cartridges, although some Confederate and imported cartridges were lubricated at the bullet end and were meant to be loaded while still wrapped in the cartridge paper.

Combustible cartridges were used extensively in carbines and revolvers. These had the bullet attached to a cartridge case made of thin nitrate paper,

Sergeant Thomas Lawrence, Company F, 22nd New York Infantry, left, and an assistant, are prepared to issue ammunition for the regiment caliber .577 Enfields. Though of British design, the Enfield was second only to the Model 1861 rifle-musket in use during the war (NA)

linen, membrane, collodion, or some other substance that would be completely consumed by the explosion of the powder. This ammunition did not need to be opened to expose the powder and was ignited by the flame from a regular percussion cap.

Separate primed cartridges, other than combustible cartridges, were best

A Confederate soldier fills his cartridge box before going into battle at a reenactment of the Battle of Corinth, Mississippi. A Civil War musket cost the government about $25. Today a reproduction of a musket costs a reenactor $600 or more. (CT)

suited for breech-loading carbines and rifles and helped the troops sustain an increased rate of fire. This type of cartridge had a case made of copper or brass, or brass and paper, or India rubber. The flame from the percussion cap penetrated through a small hole in the base of the case and ignited the powder charge. Some of these cartridges, however, were difficult to remove from the breech after firing.

The most advanced types of ammunition were those that were internally primed, such as the rimfire and the pin-fire cartridges. The rimfire cartridge contained the primer, powder, bullet, and case. The hammer of the gun struck the rim of the cartridge, igniting the fulminate and, in turn, the powder charge.

The pin-fire cartridge saw limited use. It had a brass wire "pin" that protruded through the side of the case. When struck by the hammer, the pin was driven into a percussion compound that rested on an anvil. The resulting explosion ignited the powder charge.

Ammunition for muzzleloaders was put in paper-wrapped bundles of 10 cartridges. Confederate wrappers were usually marked with the type of cartridge and the place and date of manufacture. Federal ammunition was identified on wooden packing cases for 1,000 rounds and by the color of the cartridge paper and string. Other methods of wrapping cartridges varied from pasteboard boxes to paper-covered, drilled wooden blocks.

Fitting the diameter of bullets to the caliber of weapons created problems. Muzzleloaders required bullets that were smaller than the bore diameter. Breech-loading carbines and rifles, however, used bullets larger than the bore diameter. For example, the bullet for the .52-caliber Sharps carbine was actually .535 inches in diameter, and a .44-caliber Colt bullet was .455 inches in diameter. Packages and crates were sometimes marked with the bore diameter of the weapon and at other times with the diameter of the ammunition.

The large number of calibers complicated supplying the troops. An ordnance expert explained: "Our muskets and carbines range in caliber from .40 to .61. Twenty different calibers of ammunition, from .44 to .69, were furnished in the Burnside expedition; and, lest one transport carrying all of one caliber should be lost, each vessel had to be supplied with an assorted cargo made of certain proportions of the whole."

Buck and Ball. Muskets with a .69 caliber fired a ball with three buckshot called buck and ball. As smoothbore muskets were rifled, the Minie bullet replaced this load. Buck-and-ball cartridge boxes have been found in Spotsylvania, indicating that the load was used as late as 1864.

Explosive Bullet. Both sides claimed the other used explosive bullets. Both were right. The Federal Medical Department listed 130 cases of wounds attributed to explosive bullets, and ordnance records reveal that 33,350 explosive bullets were issued to Union troops in 1863. More than 10,000 rounds were abandoned on the field and probably fell into the hands of Confederates.

The records of the 1st New Hampshire Infantry noted: "Forty rounds of cartridges per man were distributed this morning. The balls were called musket shells—an explosive bullet—and woe to the Johnny that stops one!"

One type of explosive bullet, the Gardiner bullet, had an acorn-shaped chamber fitted with fulminate, with a 1¼-second time fuse, which was ignited by the discharge of the piece. The charge was sufficient to transform the bullet into a jagged missile. If the bullet penetrated the body before exploding, its effects were even more disastrous.

Minie Ball. The Minie ball, invented by Captain Claude Etienne Minie of the French army in 1848, revolutionized warfare. The bullet was hollowed at the base for about one-third of its length. When the gun was fired, the gasses forced the lead into the rifling of the barrel. This bullet was more effective than the old .69-caliber ammunition because it was inserted into the barrel as a unit.

The Minie bullet was adopted by the U.S. army in 1855 and was used in all .58-caliber rifle-muskets. It had great stopping power. At Cold Harbor, a sergeant in the New Hampshire infantry was wounded in the right arm by a Minie bullet that shattered one bone into 23 pieces. Dug Minie balls are the most prevalent and least expensive of authentic Civil War souvenirs.

AMMUNITION BOXES. These boxes were made of white pine boards, dovetailed and nailed together, with wooden handles at the ends. The boxes were painted different colors to indicate the kind of cartridge they contained and were marked on each end with the number and kind of cartridge.

Cartridges were packed 1,000 per box. Five tiers of cartridge bundles were laid flat in a single row along each side of the box, and the rest were placed on edge, the caps alternately up and down.

APPENDAGES. Appendages are the tools and other equipment used by soldiers to disassemble, clean, and reassemble their firearms. The appendages for the rifle-muskets used by the Union army consisted of wiper, ball-screw, screwdriver, spring vise, tampion, spare cone, tumbler, and wire punch. Soldiers were forbidden to use other tools on their arms. All-purpose appendages containing all the necessary tools were developed at several arsenals. Many "Enfield" tools were imported with Enfield long arms, which were used by both the North and South.

ARMOR, BODY. Troops were not issued body armor, but some Federal soldiers bought iron vests from sutlers on the eve of their first taste of battle. One dealer reportedly sold more than 200 of these "iron-clad life preservers" in a single day to members of the 15th Connecticut Infantry.

A typical advertisement for one of these bulletproof vests claimed it had been "repeatedly and thoroughly tested with pistol bullets at 10 paces, rifle bullets at 40 rods, by army officers and approved and worn by them."

These vests were so heavy that they were soon thrown away, and the few that were used in battle failed to live up to expectations. One breastplate was worn by a Federal soldier until he was severely wounded. He then gave it to a comrade, who later was killed by a Minie ball that struck the lower part of the breastplate, passing through it and carrying pieces of the plate into the soldier's abdomen.

The breastplates worn by Federal soldiers were of two principal types. The most popular, the "Soldier's Bullet Proof Vest," was manufactured by G. and D. Cook and Co., of New Haven. It consisted of a regular black military vest containing pockets on either side of the chest into which were inserted two thin pieces of spring steel. The plates overlapped when the vest was buttoned. The infantry version of this vest weighed 3½ pounds.

A version for cavalry and artillery weighed 6 pounds.

The other type, also made by a New Haven firm, was far more complicated and cost twice as much. It consisted of four large plates held together by a keyhole and rivet system. Although these vests saved some lives, body armor passed out of use after 1862 because of its bulk and weight and the ridicule to which the wearers were subjected. Jokes about the "man in the iron stove" became popular.

ARMS, LEVER-ACTION. Lever-action arms were breech-loading firearms that employed a lever as an integral part of the arm. The lever opened the breech to allow either manual or mechanical insertion of a cartridge.

ARMS, MAGAZINE-FED. In firearms terminology, a *magazine* is an ammunition storage place and an integral part of the arm. The magazine contains a spring and a follower to automatically force one cartridge at a time into the firing chamber. Two magazine-fed arms saw extensive use in the Civil War—the Henry rifle, with its 15-cartridge magazine, and the Spencer (carbine or rifle), with its 7-cartridge magazine.

ARMS, RIFLED-BORE. Rifling in firearms consists of cutting an evenly spaced number of spiral grooves in the bore, which is the inner surface of the barrel. These grooves cause a projectile passing through the barrel to spin on its axis, which makes the projectile travel through the air without tumbling, thus greatly increasing accuracy.

ARMY AND NAVY CALIBER REVOLVERS. The terms *Army* and *Navy* can be misleading. They refer to the caliber and physical construction of the revolvers, not to the branch of the service in which the revolvers were used. Army caliber revolvers were .44 caliber, and Navy caliber revolvers were .36 caliber. It is believed that the terms originated with Samuel Colt, a master salesman, in an attempt to stimulate sales of his arms to the two branches of the service.

The Rodman gun was a Columbiad cast by a patented process that allowed larger guns to be made. A smoothbore for use in coastal fortifications, it was made in calibers of 8, 13, 15, and even 20 inches. None saw action. A few such guns were cast by the Confederates late in the war, but they were captured at the armory. (LC)

ARSENALS, CONFEDERATE. Small arms and ammunition are known to have been manufactured at the following locations in the Confederacy: Atlanta; Augusta, Georgia; Charleston; Columbus, Georgia; Columbus, Mississippi; Danville, Virginia; Fayetteville, North Carolina; Jackson, Mississippi; Little Rock; Lynchburg; Macon; Mt. Vernon, Alabama; Nashville; New Orleans; Richmond; San Antonio; Savannah; and Selma, Alabama.

ARSENALS, FEDERAL. Ordnance Department facilities at the following locations provided arms and ammunition to Federal troops.

Federal arsenals were located at Allegheny (Pittsburgh); Benicia, California; Columbus, Ohio; Fort Monroe, Virginia; Frankfort (Philadelphia); Kennebec (Augusta), Maine; Leavenworth, Kansas; St. Louis; Vancouver, Washington Territory; Washington, D.C.; Watertown, Massachusetts; and Watervliet (West Troy), New York.

Napoleon cannons like these were the most popular smoothbore fieldpieces of both North and South. By the end of the war, they had been replaced in the Union army by the new rifled cannons. (CT)

State arsenals were located at Albany; Columbus; Frankfort, Kentucky; and Indianapolis.

In addition, many private arms and ammunition makers had government contracts.

ARTILLERY FUSES. A fuse was a device for detonating a shell or case shot. Fuses were classified as time or percussion. The time fuse was composed of a case of paper, wood, or metal enclosing a burning composition. It was cut or bored to a length proportional to the intended range of the shell, so that it would detonate the bursting charge just as the shell struck or, if desired, in the air above the target. The percussion fuse exploded on impact.

In 1860, the United States used three kinds of time fuses—the mortar fuse, the Bormann fuse, and the seacoast fuse. Other types employed early in the war were the Bickford and the Gomez Patent Electric Safety fuses.

AXES AND HATCHETS. Many axes and hatchets that were used in the Union army survive today. A surprisingly large number have been found at campsites and battle sites. Axes were issued to Federal pioneer troops and units assigned to "slashing" forests in areas around fortifications. In addition, many soldiers bought hatchets from sutlers for their own use in the field.

Army Hatchets. Two types of hatchet heads have been recovered. One was a 6-inch head, measured from blade to hammer. The more common "camp hatchet" was slightly smaller with a 4⅜-inch head.

Ax Holders. Most axes were issued without holders. A typical holder was 10 inches long, 6 inches wide, and equipped with straps. Some were marked with the words "Ax Sling" and the month and year of manufacture.

Camp Ax. This ax had a wooden handle. The length of the head was 8 inches and the width of the blade, 4½ inches.

Pioneer Ax. The total length of this ax was 36 inches; the width of the bell-shaped blade from cutting edge to hammer surface was 10 inches. It had a wooden handle and no markings.

Splitting Ax. This ax had a wooden handle, painted black. Its total length was 28 inches; the length of the ax head from blade to hammer surface, 8 inches; and the width of the blade, 2¾ inches.

Reenactors "shoulder arms" before restaging the Battle of Shiloh. After the actual battle, April 6, 1862, casualty lists stunned the North. Veterans called it "Bloody Shiloh." The battle opened the way for General Grant's brilliant Vicksburg campaign. (CT)

B

BADGES, CORPS. Federal armies were composed of corps commanded by major generals. A corps at full strength numbered 25,000, but by 1863, corps in the Army of the Potomac averaged 16,000. There was no corps organization in the western theater of war until late in 1862.

Early in the war, corps badges were adopted to promote morale and for easy recognition of corps troops. Corps badges were the inspiration of General Daniel Butterfield, who designed the badges.

The 1st Army Corps badge was a disk. A trefoil, which resembled a shamrock, symbolized the 2nd Army Corps because many of its troops were Irish. A lozenge identified the 3rd Army Corps. Later, corps badges were adopted by corps in the western theater. Only 2 (the 21st and 30th) of the 25 corps failed to adopt badges.

Distribution of the badges was haphazard. Some were issued by the government, while others were purchased from sutlers or made by the troops from extra cloth.

The badges generally were made of cloth and worn on either the cap or the left side of the hat. Most metal corps badges were sold by sutlers. Some silver badges, engraved with the soldier's name, regiment, and company, were widely advertised. Whether cloth, silver, brass, or tin, corps badges actually worn in the war are scarce today.

The Confederate army did not have corps badges. Some Confederate units did adopt unit insignia, such as the distinctive badge of the Washington Artillery of New Orleans and the metal stars worn on the hats of some Texas units.

BADGES, IDENTIFICATION. Troops went into combat with little assurance that if they were killed, their bodies could be identified. Their concern was justified. In the Union, there were 184,791 men captured or missing during the war, and among the missing were thousands who were buried as "unknown." Many men who died in field hospitals were, to hospital attendants, merely bodies to be disposed of.

Sometimes men improvised means of identification. At Cold Harbor, before an obviously desperate assault, Federal soldiers calmly wrote their names and home addresses on slips of paper and pinned them on the backs of their coats.

Some Union soldiers purchased identification tags at home or from sutlers. These items were of two general types. The more expensive type, widely advertised in popular periodicals, was a pin made of gold, silver, brass, or white metal that often was quite ornate. Generally, these pins were shaped to a specific corps badge and engraved with the soldier's name or unit. Soldiers usually wore them on their coats.

The second type of marker was similar to the "dog tag" of World War II but made of brass or lead instead of aluminum. The tag had a hole for attaching a string to be worn around the neck. Usually, one side of the tag had an eagle or a shield with a phrase such as "War for the Union" or "Liberty, Union and Equality." The other side had the soldier's name or regiment.

At the beginning of the war, Federal regulations stipulated that items of equipment such as canteens, haversacks, and knapsacks be stenciled with the owner's unit number, company, and regiment. Occasionally, a soldier would scratch his name and unit on the back of the brass U.S. buckle of his belt or his leather gear.

BAYONETS, CONFEDERATE. The Confederates copied Federal bayonets. The most common was a saber bayonet designed for the Fayetteville rifle. A second type, the triangular bayonet, was made at the Richmond Armory. Most Confederate bayonets were unmarked.

Many Confederate bayonet scabbards were made locally, but many also were imported as part of the equipment used with such weapons as the Enfield from England.

The bayonet was used in battle much less than most civilians imagined. While the psychological effect of a bayonet charge was undeniable, usually one side or the other broke before the bayonets could be used effectively. Bayonets were most commonly used to pound coffee beans, to dig up vegetables, and as tenpins and candlesticks.

BAYONET, DAHLGREN. In 1856, Admiral John A. Dahlgren pointed out the need for a bowie-knife type of bayonet to be used both in hand-to-hand fighting and as a heavy tool to cut away damaged navy tackle. He devised a heavy bayonet that was adopted and used with the Plymouth rifle, another weapon manufactured according to Dahlgren's specifications. The Dahlgren bayonet became a multipurpose tool for shipboard use.

BAYONETS, FEDERAL. Several types of bayonets were used in the war, although the bayonet saw little use a weapon. The new rifle's accuracy at long ranges made bayonet charges rare occurrences. Federal soldiers, however, discovered that the bayonet was a handy tool in the field.

BAYONET, SABER. Most muskets and rifles were equipped with either socket or saber bayonets. Most Federal rifles used the socket bayonet, a needle-sharp pointed straight blade with three fluted sides. The Plymouth rifle used either a saber bayonet, which had sawteeth on one edge, or the famous Dahlgren knife bayonet. The nonregulation Merrill and Sharps rifles also were equipped with saber bayonets. However, most troops disliked the saber bayonet because it was unwieldy and added weight.

BAYONET, SAWTOOTH. This was a flat, or saber, bayonet provided with sawteeth on one edge so that it could be used as a knife or a saw. Patented in 1864, it saw little use in the war.

BIBLES. Representatives of the Christian Commission, an offshoot of the YMCA, carried Bibles to Federal troops in battle areas. During 1864 alone, the commission distributed 569,794 Bibles and Testaments; 4,815,923 hymn and song books; and 13,681,342 pages of tracts.

A Union reenactor browses in the U.S. Christian Commission tent at Gettysburg. The commission, an offshoot of the YMCA, raised $6 million to aid the troops. Besides libraries, it provided nurses in hospitals and free box lunches and coffee wagons at the front. (CT)

BOTTLES, LIQUOR. Although beer was popular among the troops, the most common intoxicant was whiskey. When the Medical Department so ordered, whiskey was supplied to enlisted men on rare occasions, such as after a strenuous march, after heavy fighting, or in rainy or snowy weather. Officers could have government whiskey whenever they wanted.

Whiskey bottles have been found in abundance at campsites. Most glass bottles were unmarked, stood 9½ inches tall, and were 2½ inches in diameter.

BREECH-LOADING. The breech-loading system allowed both projectile and gunpowder to be inserted into the firearm through the breech, or back end, of the barrel. Breech-loading significantly decreased loading time, offering a major advantage in battle. Breech-loading also allowed the shooter to load and fire with ease while he was lying down or was otherwise concealed from enemy fire. Thus, it was ideally suited to nonconventional uses, such as sharpshooting.

BUCKLES, BELT. The waist belt was fastened by a buckle, called a belt plate, that was usually oval in shape. The belt plate of the Union soldier was marked with the letters "U. S." in the center or, alternatively, with the letters of his regiment's home state ("N.Y.," for example). When the 10th Maine Infantry left for the front in 1861, they wore belt plates that were marked "V.V.M.," for Volunteer Maine Militia.

Federal noncommissioned officers wore buckles of similar shape to those of commissioned officers, but they did not have the letters identifying the wearer's branch of service.

In the Confederate army, buckles for enlisted men were rectangular and marked with the initials "C.S.A." or with state letters or seals.

Buckles have been reproduced frequently, so collectors should beware of reproductions being offered as authentic items.

BUTTONS, CONFEDERATE. Enlisted men in artillery units wore yellow buttons with a large, raised letter "A" in the center, if available. Other enlisted men wore similar buttons, except that the number of the regiment, in

These vintage bottles were recovered from the USS Cairo, *a gunboat that was sunk by mines in the Yazoo River during the siege of Vicksburg. The skeleton of the* Cairo *and the vast array of artifacts recovered from her are displayed in a special museum at the Vicksburg battlefield. (CT)*

large figures, was substituted for the letter "A."

General officers, officers of the general staff, and aides-de-camp wore bright gilt buttons with a raised spread eagle circled by stars. Other officers wore buttons indicating the branch of service—"A" for artillery, "C" for cavalry, "I" for infantry, and "R" for rifles. Officers of the Corps of Engineers wore buttons with a raised "E" in German text.

BUTTONS, FEDERAL. Early in the war, the enlisted men of many Union

An officer could wear the regulation belt plate, left, or purchase from a civilian supplier the gilt eagle plate, right. (NA)

regiments wore buttons with their state seals on them. Later, standardized buttons were used on government-issue clothing. They were yellow and showed a spread eagle with a shield superimposed on its chest.

Officers' buttons were gilt and also carried the spread eagle with the shield, but the shield contained a letter indicating the branch of service: "A" for artillery, "C" for cavalry, "D" for dragoons, "I" for infantry, "R" for rifles, and "V" for veteran volunteers. Generals and aides-de-camp wore general staff buttons, which had a spread eagle and stars with a plain border.

There also were some special buttons in the Union army. Musicians sometimes wore nonregulation buttons emblazoned with a three-string lyre. The Corps of Engineers' buttons showed an eagle holding in his beak a scroll with the word "Essayons," with a bastion with embrasures in the distance. Buttons for the Corps of Topographical Engineers had a shield on the upper half and the letters "T.E." in old English characters on the lower half.

Some collectors specialize in uniform buttons. The buttons shown here, from the Civil War Library and Museum in Philadelphia and the William L. Leigh Collection, are Union state and service buttons (the dark-colored buttons are examples of buttons made of "Goodyear's patented rubber"). The price of buttons like these ranges from a few dollars to hundreds of dollars, depending on rarity. (CWM&L)

C

CALENDARS. Combat troops often lost all track of time, even the day of the week. The only calendars were those in the pocket diaries carried by some officers, and they deteriorated in rainy weather.

Sutlers sold a permanent calendar, a thin brass disk, 1¾ inches in diameter, with seven rectangular slots and a rotating inner disk. One side of the outer disk had the months; the other side had four concentric circles with numbers from 0 to 100. By rotating the inner disk, a soldier could find the correct date of any month in a century. The calendar was marked "TIPPING'S CALENDAR" and is extremely rare.

CANDLEHOLDERS. To light his tent or hut, a soldier was issued a limited supply of candles. But neither the Union nor the Confederacy issued candleholders. Soldiers used the shanks of their bayonets to hold candles. Union soldiers also purchased privately made candleholders from sutlers.

Alexander Candleholder. Patented by Charles Alexander, of Washington, D.C. This device consisted of a socket to hold a candle in the bottom of a common tin drinking cup.

Lyman Candleholder. Patented by Alfred E. Lyman, of Williamsburg, Massachusetts. This candleholder was for use in tents. It consisted of two semi-circular parts, one of which was movable and could be adjusted at varying distances from the other by means of a set screw. It had a bracket to serve as an extension holder.

CANTEENS, CONFEDERATE. Because of the shortage of metal in the Confederacy, most canteens were made of wood by barrel makers, with some trimmed in metal. Early in the war, many rebels used clay jugs, straw- or leather-covered bottles, and various sorts of homemade "water bottles." Later, some carried imported English canteens or captured Federal canteens.

CANTEENS, FEDERAL. The regulation canteen was tin with an outer covering of cloth. It had a cork stopper with a metal cap over the top and extending down the sides, and a metal ring extending from the cork. Many Union soldiers also used nonregulation canteens that they purchased from sutlers.

CARBINES. Primarily a Union weapon, the carbine was the shoulder arm of the cavalry. Because it was intended to be carried and, if necessary, used on horseback, the average length of the Civil War carbine was 39 inches. Loading

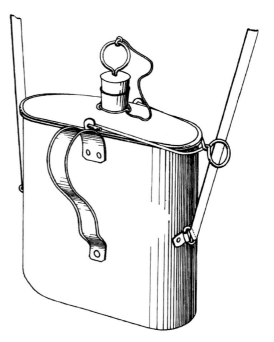

The fewer things a soldier had to carry in the field, the better. This "cooking canteen," which consisted of a bottle enclosed in a cup, could also be used to boil water. (NA)

a muzzle-loading rifle while riding a horse was difficult, and for this reason, most early breech-loading weapons were carbines. An inventor seeking to sell a new breech-loading arm had a much better chance if it were offered for cavalry use.

   Ballard Carbine. This was one of the better small-arms designs introduced during the war—a .44-caliber, single-shot breechloader employing internally primed metallic cartridges. The Ballard conquered one of the greatest failings of other metallic-cartridge arms—the ejection of the fired cartridge casing. This was accomplished by means of a manually operated, spring-loaded ejecting rod located under the breech. Once the breech was opened, the simple rearward pull of a small knob protruding through the forestock moved the rod and kicked out the casing.

Despite the effective design and quality construction of the Ballard, only 1,509 were purchased by the Federal government. However, nearly 20,000 were purchased by the state of Kentucky and issued to troops from that state.

Burnside Carbine. This was the third most widely used carbine in the Union cavalry. Beginning in 1861 and continuing throughout the war, the Federal government purchased and issued more than 50,000 .54-caliber Burnside carbines, a number exceeded only by the Spencer and the Sharps carbines.

The Burnside breech-loading mechanism was simple and effective. When the trooper lowered the operating lever, which also served as a trigger guard,

Burnside Carbine. More than 50,000 of these carbines were issued to Union troops, although some soldiers disliked them because the spent cartridge tended to stick in the breech. (USMA)

a rectangular steel block contained in the breech tilted up. This block contained a cone-shaped cavity into which a metallic cartridge of the same shape was dropped, with bullet end facing up. When the lever was closed, the block rotated forward, fitting the bullet into the chamber. Ignition was by means of a standard musket cap exploded by an external hammer. A small hole in the base of the cartridge allowed the fire to pass through.

Despite the large number of Burnside carbines issued, the arm was widely disliked. A common complaint was the weakness of the spring holding the lever shut. A second, more serious complaint was the tendency of the cartridge casing to stick in the breech block after firing.

The Burnside saw extensive use in both theaters of war, and captured Burnsides were popular with the Confederate cavalry. Toward the end of the war, the Burnside Rifle Co. received a contract for the production of Spencer carbines. The age of the externally primed cartridge was drawing to a close.

Cosmopolitan Carbine. This .52-caliber carbine was manufactured by the Cosmopolitan Arms Company, of Hamilton, Ohio, and was the only carbine purchased by the Federal government west of the Alleghenies. It had a distinctive appearance—a long, S-shaped external hammer, a scroll-like operating lever, and a barrel with no forestock.

The Cosmopolitan was operated by lowering the operating lever, which in turn caused a steel block to drop down, exposing the cartridge chamber. A cartridge was inserted and the lever closed. Ignition was by means of a standard percussion cap.

Beginning in June 1862, the Federal government purchased more than 9,000 Cosmopolitans. Many who were issued these carbines felt they were satisfactory, but several regiments raised serious objections. The 8th Ohio Cavalry felt the Cosmopolitan to be "an inefficient and unreliable weapon." Among the objections were these: "The carbine does not carry to the sights (in other words, it is inaccurate). After a few discharges it leaks fire. The least jar will break some of its parts or the stock." These and other objections were sustained by one chief ordnance officer, who condemned the Cosmopolitan as "a very worthless weapon . . . thrust upon the Ordnance Department by political influence of contractors."

C.S. Sharps Carbine. Confederate arms manufacturers copied the simple mechanism of the Sharps carbine used by the North. The S. C. Robinson Co., of Richmond, and the Confederate government produced some 5,000 C.S. Sharps carbines that were nearly identical to their Northern counterpart. The failing of the C.S. Sharps came in the quality of manufacture, which resulted in a weapon prone to malfunctions in the field.

Gallager Carbine. This .50-caliber weapon was the invention of Mahlon

C.S. Richmond Cavalry Carbine. Breech-loading carbines were the hardest weapons to come by in the Confederacy, and many cavalrymen carried rifles or sawed-off shotguns instead. Some 5,000 of this .56-caliber carbine were produced at the Richmond Armory on machinery captured from the Harpers Ferry arsenal. (USMA)

J. Gallager, of Savannah, but despite its Southern heritage, it was manufactured in Philadelphia and is numbered among the various types issued to the Union cavalry.

The Gallager employed a breech-loading mechanism that consisted of a lever/trigger-guard combination that, when pushed down, allowed the barrel to slide forward and tilt up and away from the breech. The brass-cased cartridge was then inserted directly into the breech end of the barrel itself. Raising the lever repositioned the barrel and seated the base of the cartridge into the breech. For ignition, a standard musket cap was exploded by an external hammer.

Nearly 18,000 Gallager carbines were issued to Union troops during the war. The weapon, though, was not well liked, due primarily to difficulty removing the cartridge casing from the breech after firing.

Gibbs Carbine. This .52-caliber carbine saw only very limited service in the war. Only 1,050 Gibbs carbines were purchased by the Federal government before a fire destroyed the factory. About half of the small production was sent to the Army of the Potomac, the rest to Missouri.

The Gibbs mechanism was simple. The soldier lowered the operating lever/trigger guard, which caused the barrel to slide forward a short distance and tip upward. He then inserted a linen cartridge into the barrel chamber. Reversing the motion closed the breech and seated the cartridge. In August

1863, a Union ordnance officer reported: "I cannot report favorably on the arm. The working is very simple but perfectly exposed, rending it liable to catch all dirt and the smallest stick or pebble getting into it renders it unserviceable, until it is taken apart and cleaned."

Keen, Walker & Co. Carbine. Only some 200 of these well-crafted Confederate .52-caliber carbines were produced during the war. (USMA)

Hall Model 1843 Carbine. This carbine preceded the war by 18 years and, moreover, was itself a modification of a design in use since 1833. The .52-caliber Hall employed a rising breech block that was activated by a lever located on the right side of the arm above the trigger. Pressure on the lever caused the carbine breech to tilt upward, allowing the soldier to place a paper cartridge into the breech. Repositioning the lever closed the breech and aligned the bullet with the barrel. For ignition, a standard musket cap was struck by a hammer contained in the breech block.

The Federal cavalry used about 5,000 Halls in the western theater, mostly with Illinois and Missouri cavalrymen. In the East, the Hall saw service, at least through 1863, with General J. E. B. Stuart's cavalry of the Army of Northern Virginia. This is documented by ordnance returns for several regiments, including the famed 1st Virginia Cavalry.

Maynard Carbine. This .50-caliber carbine was one of the most accurate breech-loading carbines produced during the war. Despite its small size and comparatively light weight (6 pounds), it was rugged and well made.

The loading mechanism employed an operating lever/trigger guard. When this was pivoted down, the barrel raised to allow the insertion of a special metallic cartridge with an extrawide base. Reversal of the loading procedure repositioned the barrel. The wide base of the cartridge acted as a seal to prevent the loss of explosive force when the gun was fired. This extrawide base made the fired cartridge easy to pull from the chamber. Ignition of the cartridge was by means of a standard musket cap exploded by an exposed hammer that was contained in the breech. The fire from the discharge of the cap passed through a small hole in the cartridge base.

Several models of the Maynard carbine were used in the war, but all functioned basically the same way. The first model, manufactured before the war, had a target-quality rear sight, and 2,369 of these were produced. No Maynards were purchased by the Federal government until June 1864. These later Maynards had standard military sights but saw only limited service.

Merrill Carbine. The same unique top-opening loading mechanism employed in the Merrill rifle was used in this carbine. To load the carbine, the trooper raised a lever on top of the carbine breech, exposing the cartridge chamber. He then inserted a paper cartridge. When he closed the lever, a small piston contained in a track behind the chamber pushed the cartridge forward and seated the bullet. The cartridge was fired by means of a standard musket cap ignited by an external hammer.

The .54-caliber Merrill carbine was never popular, although more than 15,000 were issued to Union cavalry beginning in 1861. By mid-1863, those still in use were concentrated in the western theater of the war, with only a very few in use by cavalrymen in the Army of the Potomac.

Because of the early issue of Merrill carbines, a number were captured by Confederate cavalry, and their use by Southern horsemen was common. Requisitions for Merrill ammunition were often contained in the official correspondence of Army of Northern Virginia cavalry regiments.

Model 1855 Pistol-Carbine. This unusual weapon was a .58-caliber, single-shot muzzle-loading percussion handgun that was equipped with a separate shoulder stock. The stock, when attached to the handgrip of the pistol, effectively converted the pistol to a carbine. Thus, the gun could be fired from the shoulder, increasing stability and accuracy.

The pistol-carbine fired virtually the same ammunition as the 1855 rifle-musket. Like the rifle-musket, it achieved ignition by the new Maynard primer. A total of 4,021 of these weapons were produced by the Springfield Armory in Massachusetts during 1855 and 1856.

The pistol-carbine was a well-made weapon, but it was obsolete from the time it went into production. The six-shot revolver manufactured by the Colt Firearms Company of Hartford, was the gun of the future. But the arms shortage brought on by the war forced some early volunteers to use the pistol-carbine until it was replaced by a more conventional weapon.

Sharps Carbine. For nearly a decade before the war, Sharps carbines were known as rugged and efficient arms. The first Sharps used by U.S. forces were issued in 1854, and from then until the end of the Civil War, they proved their value in every major cavalry action.

The Sharps carbine, like the Sharps rifle, used a paper or a linen cartridge and fired a .52-caliber bullet. The Sharps carbine and rifle were mechanically identical. By means of a lever, which also served as a trigger guard, the soldier opened the carbine breech and loaded a single cartridge.

Union and Confederate cavalrymen liked the Sharps carbine, and many favored it over more advanced arms. One Union ordnance officer reported: "A cavalry carbine should be very simple in its mechanism, with all its . . . parts well covered from the splashing of mud, or the accumulation of rust and dust. Sharps carbines combine all these estimable qualities."

Sharps Model 1863 Carbine. The Sharps stood up well under hard use and cost less to make than the technically superior Henry. (USMA)

Smith Carbine. Beginning in January 1862, more than 31,000 Smith carbines were purchased by the Federal government, and they ranked fourth in number issued to Union cavalry troops.

The .50-caliber Smith carbine, manufactured by Poultney and Trimble, of Baltimore, employed a unique but simple breech-loading system. An upward pressure on a brass plunger located in front of the trigger raised a spring-steel strap on the top of the barrel. This released the barrel, which then pivoted down and away from the breech. The cartridge was inserted into the chamber at the rear of the barrel. When the barrel was pivoted back into position, the base of the cartridge fit into the carbine breech. Ignition was achieved by a musket cap exploded by an external hammer.

The Smith was originally designed to use a cartridge with a hard rubber case. As with several other carbines, the greatest objection to the Smith was the difficulty often encountered in extracting the cartridge case after firing. Early in the war, many Smiths fell into the hands of Southern cavalrymen, and frequent requisitions for Smith ammunition have been found in Confederate Ordnance Department correspondence.

Spencer Carbine. Although not issued until October 1863, the Spencer carbine proved to be the most popular and widely used U.S. cavalry shoulder arm of the war.

The Spencer carbine functioned exactly the same as its predecessor, the Spencer rifle, and used the same rimfire metallic cartridge; but at 39 inches, it was 8 inches shorter than the rifle. Both arms were lever-action, .52-caliber repeaters with a seven-round tubular magazine contained in the buttstock.

The development of the Spencer carbine was a direct result of reports such as the following from a cavalry ordnance officer: "The Spencer Repeating Rifle is used by the 5th and 6th Michigan Cavalry and is very highly spoken of by officers and men in those commands, [but] as a rifle it is too heavy for the mounted service and is now used by those commands on foot mostly as skirmishers. I would recommend a similar arm with the barrel shortened to the size and weight of a carbine as the best arm for the cavalry service. A metallic cartridge is undoubtedly the best for cavalry, as a large amount of ammunition is wasted by jolting the cartridge boxes, or becomes wet with rain or the fording of rivers. The Spencer cartridge contains within itself a perfect gas check and cap, and can be fired eight times without taking it from the shoulder, one cartridge in the barrel and seven in the stock. The mechanism is very simple and tightly covered from dirt or rust. As a rifle it has had a thorough test in the field and is very popular."

In total, more than 95,000 Spencer carbines were purchased by the Federal government. As with all other arms issued to Union troops, some Spencers were captured and used by Confederates. However, the unique rimfire cartridge of the Spencer proved too expensive and difficult for Confederate manufacturing facilities to produce. The need to rely solely on captured ammunition limited the use of the Spencer by Southern cavalrymen.

Starr Carbine. Similar in appearance and function to the Sharps, the Starr carbine did not approach the quality of its famous look-alike. The .54-caliber Starr employed a dropping-block action that was activated by the downward motion of the operating lever/trigger guard. This caused a block in the breech to drop below the rear of the barrel. The trooper then inserted a linen-cased cartridge into the barrel chamber. The reverse movement of the lever closed the breech. Ignition was achieved by a musket cap and external hammer.

The Federal government purchased more than 20,000 Starrs during the war, but the carbine was not well liked. In 1863, a Union ordnance officer reported: "Starr's carbine . . . is an evasion of Sharps patent with none of its virtues. The mechanism, too light and complicated, works well enough while perfectly new but the least dirt deranges it. It requires both hands to press back the lever, the cartridge is not readily placed straight in the barrel, and the gas check is very imperfect. After a few firings the saltpeter corrodes the barrel where it enters the gas check, rendering the lever doubly hard to open. As the part becomes more corroded, the effect of the discharge would be greatly impaired. When this occurs, it could only be mended by a new barrel and new gas check."

CAVALRY ARMS AND EQUIPMENT. At first, Federal cavalry units had no standard firearms. Some troopers were equipped with Hall carbines, an inferior gun of limited range. A few men had Colt Navy revolvers, while others were issued clumsy Austrian infantry rifles, which many of them "lost."

In contrast, the Federal cavalry was overloaded with equipment—blankets, brushes, canteens, cartridges, coffeepots, cups, currycombs, frying pans, haversacks, lariats, nose bags, picket pins, sabers and belts, spurs, and watering bridles. When a regiment attempted to mount, wrote one observer, "such a rattling, jangling, jerking, scrabbling, cursing was never heard before."

Confederate cavalrymen preferred the revolver over the saber. Many also carried short Enfield rifles and musketoons, cut-down infantry muskets, sporting rifles, and shotguns.

As for equipment, Confederate troopers used whatever was at hand. The marked superiority of the Confederate cavalry through June 1863 was due, in large measure, to its superior mobility. Unlike their opponents, Confederate cavalrymen were not overloaded with unnecessary equipment.

CHAPEAUS DE BRAS. The chapeau de bras was a dress hat, worn mainly by Federal naval officers, that could be folded and carried under the arm. Although these hats were no longer regulation cover in the Union army, Winfield Scott and a few other generals continued to wear chapeaus de bras. Chapeaus were not used in the Confederate service.

CHEVRONS. The rank of a noncommissioned officer in the Union army was indicated by chevrons, worn pointed down, above the elbows of both sleeves of the uniform coat and overcoat. Chevrons were made of silk or worsted binding, ½ inch wide, and they were either yellow, the same color as the edging of the coat, or the color of the branch of the army.

A corporal wore two bars; a sergeant, three bars; a first sergeant, three bars and a lozenge; an ordnance sergeant, three bars and a tie; and a sergeant major, three bars in an arc. Soldiers in pioneer units wore crossed hatchets. Hospital stewards wore a half chevron of emerald green with a caduceus of yellow embroidered on it.

Chevrons also indicated length of service of noncommissioned officers, privates, and musicians. Those who had served faithfully for five years wore

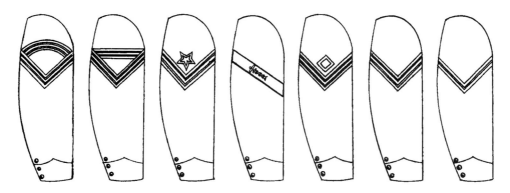

In the Union army, chevrons, worn above the elbow on both sleeves, denoted rank and, in most cases, the wearer's specialty. From left: sergeant major, quartermaster sergeant, ordnance sergeant, hospital steward, first sergeant, sergeant, and corporal. (NA)

a diagonal half chevron below the elbow on both sleeves. An additional half chevron was added above the first for each subsequent five years. Wartime service was indicated by a sky blue strip on each side of the chevron for artillery and a red strip for all other branches.

Confederate army chevrons designated the same ranks as in the Federal army.

COEHORN MORTAR. One of the most useful weapons of the war was also one of the least known. The Coehorn mortar, named for Baron Van Coehorn, the Dutch military engineer who invented it, was easily manned and adjusted, used very little powder, and was effective in siege operations. Curiously, this small, portable mortar, used successfully in the Mexican War, was not used in the Civil War to any extent until 1864. It was used only by the North.

The Coehorn threw a 24-pound shell to a distance of 1,200 yards, using ½ pound of powder. It weighed 164 pounds, and two men could carry it easily. It was used against enemy personnel who were sheltered from the fire of fieldpieces by sloping terrain. The best defense against the Coehorn was the "bombproof," a shelter used around Petersburg and Richmond. A bombproof was made of logs heavily banked with dirt. Some were built above ground, while others were holes in the ground.

CONTAINERS, POWDER. Most ammunition used in the Civil War was fixed, but there was some use of canned powder. Powder was stored in barrels, both metal and wood.

Metal Powder Barrel. This container was made of tin, measured 11½ inches tall and 9¼ inches in diameter, and was painted green and red. A metal stopper for the hole at the top of the barrel was marked "Patent July 12, 1859." A paper pasted on the bottom of the barrel bore the inscription "Hazard Powder Company, Hazardville, Conn. U.S. Government Warranted proof. Cannon." The paper also had a design of crossed cannons.

Wood Powder Barrel. This container was 13 inches tall and 10½ inches in diameter. It was wrapped top and bottom with wooden strips, four at each end. The top had a wooden plug that screwed into the hole for emptying powder from the barrel. The top of the barrel was marked "FFF GLAZED" and "10821 E," while the bottom was marked "Laflin and Rand Powder Co. New York."

E

ENTRENCHING TOOLS. Union and Confederate soldiers on work detail and in pioneer troops were furnished with saws, felling axes, spades, mattocks, pickaxes, and bell hooks. U.S. army regulations defined pioneers as "working parties attached to convoys to mend roads, remove obstacles, and erect defenses. The convoys should always be provided with spare wheels, poles, axles, etc."

Line troops, often whole regiments, were detailed to work on fortifications and to prepare their own positions for defense in combat. Such troops were issued entrenching tools.

Artillery Shovel. This tool was 4 feet 6¾ inches long overall. A ring was attached to the handle at a point 9 inches from the end.

Spade. This was shorter than the artillery shovel and was more commonly used because it was better adapted to field service. The spade was 3 feet long, and the spade proper was 7 inches wide. All metal parts were painted black.

EPAULETTES, DRESS. All Union officers were required to wear an epaulette on each shoulder, with the following exceptions: when they were not on duty and when they were on the march, unless there was an immediate expectation of meeting the enemy. In fact, most officers in the field wore shoulder boards rather than dress epaulettes to indicate rank.

The epaulette for a general officer was made of gold cloth, with a solid crescent. The insignia of rank was worn on the strap, with the stars embroidered in silver.

In addition to insignia of rank, regimental officers wore their regimental numbers embroidered in gold, within a circlet of embroidered silver, on cloth of the following colors: artillery, scarlet; cavalry, yellow; and infantry, light blue.

Staff officers also wore letters or emblems on their epaulettes, denoting branch of service: engineers—a turreted castle of silver; topographical engineers—a shield embroidered in gold with the Old English letters "T.E."; medical— a laurel wreath in gold with the Old English letters "M.S."; ordnance—a shell and flame in silver; and pay—the same as for medical but with the letters "P.D."

Confederate army officers had a similar system of dress epaulettes.

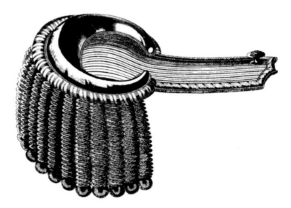

Epaulettes were worn on the shoulders of the frock coat of an army officer, except for certain designated occasions. It is difficult to imagine the thousands of miles of gold braid used in officers' uniforms during the war. (NA)

F

FARRIER'S TOOLS. Both armies used horses extensively. In addition to cavalry and artillery units, field grade officers, from infantry majors to commanding generals, also were mounted. Thousands of draft horses and mules were necessary for the wagon trains. Thus, it was essential to have blacksmiths in sufficient numbers to keep these horses and mules clipped and well shod. In the military, blacksmiths were known as farriers. Farriers' tools included the following.

Farrier's Knife. This tool, measuring 2⅝ inches long, was used to pare the hoof to fit the shoe. The hook on the knife was helpful in removing stones and other objects that became caught in the hoof.

The Civil War depended on horses, and farriers, as military blacksmiths were called, kept the horses and mules well shod. Farriers and their equipment, including a portable forge, traveled with their regiments. As soon as a halt was called at day's end, the forge was fired up and the farrier ready for action. (LC)

Hair Clippers. These 12-inch clippers looked and worked like modern grass clippers.

Tongs. The farrier's 12-inch tongs were made of heavy steel to clip off the ends of nails driven in to hold the shoe on the hoof.

FIELD ARTILLERY EQUIPMENT. This equipment included all the devices for laying and firing the pieces and for loading, cleaning, and repairing the weapons, in addition to miscellaneous tools and articles used in the battery. Only a few of these devices, however, are of interest to collectors.

Ammunition Chest. For the 6-pounder gun, a chest carried 50 rounds: 25 fixed shot, 20 fixed spherical case shot, 5 fixed canisters, 2 spare cartridges, 75 friction primers, 2 yards of slow-match, and 2 portfires. When full, the chest weighed 376 pounds.

Caisson. A caisson was an ammunition cart for mobile artillery. When coupled to its limber, the caisson became a four-wheeled vehicle. The number of caissons with field batteries varied: with a battery of 12-pounders, eight caissons for guns and four for howitzers; with a battery of 6-pounders, four for guns and two for howitzers.

Cannon Sight. This was a pendulum sight having two graduated standard bars and one sliding extension bar between the standards, resembling the letter T.

Gun Carriage Equipment. This equipment included a felling ax, a pickax, a long-handled shovel, a spare handspike, a spare pole, a spare wheel, a tar bucket, a large tarpaulin, two hooks, and two leather watering buckets.

Limber. Often confused with the caisson, the limber was a two-wheeled vehicle similar in general appearance to the caisson; however, instead of carrying projectiles, the "chest" contained tools and items necessary for firing the cannon. When the battery was actually firing, the limber was about 10 yards behind the cannon. The gun limber was the lead part of a mobile gun carriage to which horses were attached.

Quadrant. This wood or metal device was used with mortars and long artillery pieces, for which the ordinary breech sight and tangent were insufficient.

FLAGS, COLORS, STANDARDS, AND GUIDONS, FEDERAL. In the U.S. military service, there were various names for flags, including flag, colors, standard, and guidon. *Flag* was a general term, applicable regardless of size or use, but usually it applied only to flags displayed from buildings, not those carried by troops. The other terms refer to specific uses: *Colors,* during the Civil War, were the national, state, or regimental flags carried by dismounted units; a *standard* was the flag carried by mounted units; and a *guidon* was a small flag carried by a military unit as a unit marker.

When the war came, the U.S. flag had 33 stars. The arrangement of these stars varied greatly, including such patterns as a huge star or an anchor. The flag over Fort Sumter in April 1861 had a star arrangement of seven vertical lines (5-3-5-7-5-3-5), although the most common arrangement was five horizontal lines of stars (7-7-5-7-7).

Today, colors and standards are used by troops only during ceremonies, but during the Civil War, they also were carried into battle. Each regiment had a color guard composed of men of exceptionally fine physique and demonstrated courage. The guard usually consisted of four or more men, two carrying the colors and at least two acting as guards. The colors served as a rallying point for the regiment.

Battle Streamers. The War Department ruled that units would carry streamers, attached to the flag staff, bearing the names of the battles in which they were participants. The order read in part: "It is expected that troops so distinguished will regard their colors as representing the honor of their corps— to be lost only with their lives; and ... those not yet entitled to such a distinction will not rest satisfied until they have won it by their discipline and courage." In actual practice, the names of battles were painted on unit flags in lieu of battle streamers being issued.

Camp Colors. Camp colors were made of bunting, 18 inches square, white for infantry and red for artillery, with the number of the regiment on them. The pole was 8 feet long.

Garrison Flag. The garrison flag was the national flag, made of bunting, 30 feet wide by 20 feet high.

Guidon. The guidon was swallow-tailed, 3 feet 5 inches from the lance to the end of the swallowtail and 2 feet 3 inches on the lance. The guidon was half red and half white, dividing at the fork, with the red on top. On the red were the letters "U.S." in white, and on the white was the letter of the company in red.

Headquarters Flags. The Union army had distinctive headquarters flags for corps, divisions, and brigades. The flags of army corps carried the insignia of the corps. Divisions were indicated by colors: first division, red; second, white; third, blue; and fourth, green. Brigades were indicated by numerical designations.

Hospital Flags. In January 1864, the War Department established distinctive hospital and ambulance flags, as follows: general hospitals, yellow bunting, 9 by 5 feet, with the letter "H" in green bunting in the center; post and field hospitals, yellow bunting, 6 by 4 feet, also with the letter "H" in green bunting; and ambulances, yellow bunting, 29 by 24 inches, with a 1-inch-wide green border.

Mounted Regiment Standards and Guidons. Each regiment was provided with a silk standard, and each company with a silk guidon. The standard bore the arms of the United States embroidered in silk on a blue ground, with the number and name of the regiment in a scroll beneath the eagle. The standard was 2 feet 5 inches wide and was edged in yellow silk fringe. The guidon was a smaller version of the silk standard.

Regular Army Colors. An infantry regiment had two silken colors. The national color had the number and name of the regiment embroidered in silver on the center stripe. The regimental color was blue, with the arms of the United States embroidered in silk on the center; the name of the regiment was on a scroll, beneath the eagle. The color was 6 feet 6 inches wide and 6 feet deep on the pike. The pike, including spear and ferrule, was 9 feet 10 inches. The fringe was yellow, while the cords and tassels were blue and white silk intermixed.

An artillery regiment also had two silken colors. The national color had the number and name of the regiment embroidered in gold on the center stripe. The regimental color was yellow, had the same dimensions as the regiment's national color, and bore in the center two crossed cannons, with

A regular army unit, the 1st Battalion, 11th U.S. Infantry, was awarded this presentation flag for long and faithful service during the war. The names of battles sewn onto the flag show the unit went through the Peninsula campaign, then fought in most of the important battles of the war, right up to Lee's surrender at Appomattox. (USMA)

the letters "U.S." above, the number of the regiment below. The fringe was yellow. The color and pike were of the same dimensions as those carried by infantry regiments. The cords and tassels were red and yellow silk intermixed.

Volunteer and Militia Colors. State regimental colors differed from regular army colors in that the coat of arms of the United States was replaced by the state coat of arms. State regimental colors were generally presented to the regiment in impressive ceremonies just before the regiment left for the war. The colonel in command would give a speech of appreciation, assuring the donors that the regiment would guard the colors with their lives. Most of these colors were beautiful and extremely expensive.

This South Carolina state seal flag was carried in combat by Company B, 5th Regiment, South Carolina Infantry. Companies used their flags as visual rallying points on the battlefield. An enlisted man considered it a high honor to carry the company flag, and many died protecting the flag. It was a coup to capture a company flag, a disgrace to lose one's own. (MOC)

FLAGS, CONFEDERATE. The Confederacy had four flags. The first, adopted March 4, 1861, consisted of two horizontal red stripes with a white stripe between them and seven white stars in a circle on a blue field. At First Manassas, the first large land battle of the war, the Confederates found that this flag was easily confused with the Stars and Stripes. A second flag was then adopted—red with a blue St. Andrew's cross containing 13 white stars.

Shortly after the Confederacy was formed, a design competition was held to choose a national flag. Some of the losing entries were displayed 125 years later at the Library of Congress. (JW)

A Confederate national flag was adopted May 1, 1863, to replace the Stars and Bars. This new flag was white, with the battle flag (Stars and Bars) in the upper right quarter.

A fourth flag, adopted March 4, 1865, was created by adding a broad vertical bar to the edge of the national flag. This was done because, when furled, the old national flag showed too much white and resembled a flag of truce or surrender.

Some Confederate states in the West had no traditional state flags and did not authorize official state battle colors until after the outbreak of hostilities. As a result, soldiers from these states turned to the first Confederate national flag as a model for their regimental colors. These flags varied according to the tastes and capabilities of the makers. The arrangement of stars differed from flag to flag. Most of these flags were replaced, though a few were carried until late in the war.

FOOD. Hardtack was a plain flour-and-water biscuit supplied to troops on both sides. Officially called hard bread, the biscuit had small holes in it and resembled today's saltines. Nine of these biscuits constituted a ration in some regiments, 10 in others. Soldiers complained that hardtack was often wormy, wet, or moldy.

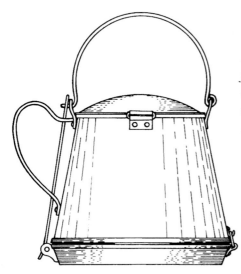

Blakeslee's mess kit featured a detachable frying pan affixed to the bottom of a camp coffeepot. Sometimes it seemed as if every tinkerer in the country had an idea and was trying to sell it to the army. (NA)

Today's soldier would feel at home in this mess hall of a permanent training camp in the Washington, D.C. area. The decorations suggest that Christmas dinner is about to be served. Army food in the field was poor by modern standards but a banquet compared with the rations of the Confederate soldier. (NA)

Hardtack was put up in wooden boxes. It was a common sight to see thousands of boxes of hardtack piled up at railroad stations, left exposed to the elements. It is a tribute to the durability of hardtack that biscuits can be seen in museums and private collections today.

Soldiers devised ways to make hardtack more palatable. Many soaked hardtack in coffee, and this often constituted the soldier's entire meal, especially in the field. Some crumbled the hardtack in cold water and then fried the crumbs in the juice and fat of meat. A dish called Skillygalee was prepared by soaking hardtack in cold water, then frying it in pork fat. Others toasted their hardtack until it was charred, in the belief that well-toasted hardtack was good for weak bowels.

Instant coffee was introduced during the Civil War to make a soldier's rations less bulky. It was prepared in paste form and contained milk and sugar. One report said that General Grant tested instant coffee before it was first issued to his troops.

Coffee and sugar rations were sometimes issued in small cotton bags, and a haversack could become odorous with its mixture of bacon, pork, sugar, coffee, tea, desiccated vegetables, rice, bits of yesterday's dinner, and old scraps husbanded against a day of want.

Hardtack and tobacco—two staples of the Civil War soldier's russet bag—are evidenced among this assortment of original relics. (SB)

G

GAMES. During long, boring days in camp, soldiers on both sides played various games to pass the time.

Checkers and Chess. Checkers was a favorite game, while chess was rarely played except by officers. Usually, the higher the educational level of the soldier, the more apt he was to play chess.

Chuck-or-Luck. After the troops had been paid, their Chuck-or-Luck banks would appear as if by magic. At each bank, there would be 10 to 20 men, all down on their knees, placing their money on certain figures laid out on a board or, more often, on a rubber blanket, while a "banker" threw the dice. Officers played a similar game called Sweat-Board. Dice were crude and much smaller than dice in use today.

Dominoes. Dominoes were popular, and the pieces were usually made by the soldiers themselves.

Playing Cards. Various card games, such as cribbage and euchre, were popular with both Union and Confederate soldiers, and it was common to play for money. Poker was a great favorite. At various headquarters, army down to brigade, the game drew in staff officers who frequently won—or lost—several months' pay in a single session. In the 150th Pennsylvania Infantry, the game became an "absorbing occupation, the private soldier yielding to its fascinations as readily as his superiors, and risking his scanty allowance as heedlessly as the latter their liberal stipend."

One deck of cards commonly used by Union soldiers was the American Card Company's "Union Playing Cards," consisting of the following suits: Eagles, Shields, Stars, and Flags. A colonel stood for a king, the Goddess of Liberty for a queen, and a major for a jack.

Confederate playing cards had a stand-of-arms design; individual cards bore a portrait of a different Confederate general or cabinet member.

Prison Games. In prison camps, the men improvised games. Federal

Games, including cribbage, chess, and horseshoes passed the soldier's time. Pieces such as these attract collectors of Civil War artifacts and vintage novelties alike. (SB)

officers at Belle Isle played chess, dominoes, checkers, and cards. Chess was played on a grid marked out on the floor, with chessmen made of beef bones. Dominoes and checkers were played in a like manner, with buttons and wooden men. Games of cards played on constantly, especially euchre, whist, and bluff. The greasy, worn cards were guarded carefully, as they were invaluable to men desperately in need of recreation.

GRENADES, HAND. Both sides used hand grenades in siege operations. At Vicksburg, the Confederates filled glass bottles with powder and balls with fuses in the open ends. At Port Hudson, Federal troops improvised hand grenades from 6-pound shells. While defending fortifications, soldiers could throw the smaller grenades by hand into a trench or covered way or upon attackers mounting a breach in the works. The larger grenades could be rolled over the parapet into the defender's trench.

In the 1863 Federal assault on Port Hudson, the skirmishers were deployed at intervals of two paces and were followed by five companies armed with hand grenades. The order for the attack specified: "The hand grenade men carry their pieces on their backs and carry each one grenade. They will march three paces in rear of their line of skirmishers. The skirmishers will clamber up on the parapet followed by the carriers of hand grenades, which will be thrown over into the works as soon as the skirmishers are on the outer slopes of the parapets."

The Confederates reported that the results were unsuccessful. In some instances, the Federal skirmishers succeeded in getting to the trenches and throwing their grenades over the parapets. But many grenades failed to explode or were thrown back at the assaulting forces. The entire engagement lasted about four hours, with heavy losses to the attackers.

Adams Hand Grenade. A primer was attached to the time fuse inserted in the grenade. When the grenade was thrown, the primer was activated and thus ignited the time fuse.

Hanes "Excelsior" Hand Grenade. This grenade was a cast-iron sphere with inner and outer shells. The inner shell contained the powder, and on its outside were screwed 14 nipples that took regular musket percussion caps. The outer shell was separated from the inner shell by a cushion to prevent the caps from prematurely coming into contact with the outside shell. When the grenade struck an object, at least one of the caps was sure to explode the shell. Since the outer shell was in two parts, these parts would break into many destructive fragments. The grenade was so dangerous to handle, however, that only a few were ever manufactured.

Ketchum Hand Grenade. This was the most common grenade of the Civil War. It had an elongated form and bulged at the center. An opening at one end was fitted with a tube of soft metal with a flange at the outer end and a nipple for holding a percussion cap. The charge was then placed in the shell, and when the grenade was to be used, a stick with four wings of pasteboard was inserted in the end opposite the cap. The wings helped guide the grenade, like the tail of a kite. In the cap tube was a plunger that exploded the cap when it struck something. To prevent accidental discharge, soldiers did not insert the plunger until just before throwing the grenade.

GUN SLINGS. Gun slings were issued to soldiers on both sides, though many period photographs show men with muskets not equipped with slings. There were three main types of slings.

Many Confederates used a sling made of light canvas, with two leather loops and a heavy wire hook on the end. Many also used the Enfield gun sling. This standard British–issue sling was imported for use with the Enfield and came in both russet and buff leathers.

The U.S. gun sling was made of russet leather, with two loops and a brass hook on the end. The sling was modified to accommodate the various types of shoulder arms in use.

H

HAVELOCK. The havelock was a simple white linen covering for the cap, with an attached cape to protect the neck from the sun. It was named for British General Henry Havelock, who distinguished himself in the war in India in 1857, where this covering was worn.

Havelocks may have been essential to the comfort of British troops in India, and whole Union regiments went to war with them in 1861; but they never proved their value in the Civil War, and few survived prolonged active service. Those that were not thrown away were put to use as patches for cleaning the bores of rifles and muskets. Havelocks were much publicized in the North early in the war, and the folks at home enthusiastically made them for their soldiers.

HAVERSACKS, CONFEDERATE. Confederates usually carried a simple homemade affair of white linen or cotton, in which they stored their meager allowance of corn pone or goober peas. They also used captured Union haversacks and those brought through the blockade.

Few Confederate haversacks have survived, probably because of their utilitarian value. Many were used after the war by school children to carry books and by adults for use around the farm or home. One was found hanging in a barn, filled with clothespins.

HAVERSACKS, FEDERAL. A Union soldier in the field carried his rations in a haversack made of canvas, oilcloth, leather, or a combination of these. A tin cup was attached to the outside.

Many officers purchased haversacks of elaborate design, often made of patent leather, which would hold only one day's rations. These had a convenient pocket in which the officer might carry a flask of whiskey—for medicinal purposes—while his reserve supplies were transported by wagon or on the shoulders of his servant, usually a loyal and rugged "contraband" (a former slave).

Regulation haversacks were usually marked with the number and name of the regiment, the company letter, and the soldier's company number. Regulation haversacks were better made than ones sold by private firms; they had an inside lining that kept the rations from coming into contact with the haversack itself.

Haversacks in museums and private collections suggest that there were two main types issued to troops—canvas and black oilcloth.

All haversacks were waterproof in theory, but once they became worn, they were no better than ordinary cloth for keeping water out. A penetrating rain would make a mess of the contents. The canvas types were white when issued, but once in active service, they shortly turned black.

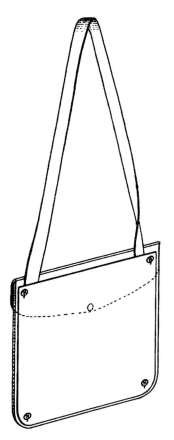

Soldiers, North and South, carried their field rations in a haversack slung over the right shoulder. Keech's haversack, patented in 1863, was made of duck cloth and featured a detachable waterproof side piece to keep food from soaking through and staining the soldier's uniform. (NA)

One Union soldier wrote: "By the time one of these [white canvas haversacks] had been in use for a few weeks as a receptacle for chunks of fat, bacon, and fresh meat, damp sugar tied up in a rag—perhaps a piece of an old shirt— potatoes, and other vegetables that might be picked up along the route, it took on the color of a printing office towel. It would have been alike offensive to the eyes and nose of a fastidious person."

A veteran was accustomed to the looks and odors of his haversack. At the halt, he would drop by the roadside, draw his grimy and well-greased haversack around in front of him, and begin to eat from it.

HOLSTERS, PISTOL. Two types of holsters were in general use both North and South—those worn on the belt and the double holsters used by mounted men, which attached to the saddle pommel. The belt holsters varied according to the size and model of the pistol or revolver that they held.

HORSE EQUIPMENT. Federal troops generally used the following horse equipment.

Artillery Valise. Made of black bridle leather, this large travel bag had a heavy leather flap extended well over the front of the valise. The valise was lined with denim and had leather carrying handles and three straps on the cover. Each end of the valise was marked with wording such as "U.S. Watervliet Arsenal, G. "

Bridoon. This was the snaffle and rein of a military bridle that acted independently of the bit, at the control of the rider.

Horse Furniture. Regulations specified that for general officers, a housing of dark blue cloth be worn over the saddle, trimmed with two rows of gold lace. At each corner were ornaments to denote the rider's rank. Major generals who commanded armies had a gold embroidered spread eagle and three stars. Other major generals had a spread eagle but only two stars. Brigadier generals had the eagle and one star.

Mounted Troops Equipment. A complete set of horse equipment for mounted troops consisted of bridle, currycomb, halter, horse brush, picket pin, saddle, saddlebags, saddle blanket, spurs, surcingle, and watering bridle.

Clad in Confederate gray, a reenactor pauses before his tent at the Wilson's Creek National Battlefield in Missouri. Actually, rebels wore uniforms of butternut, light and dark brown, and gray so dark it could be mistaken for Union blue. (CT)

When required, a link and a nose bag also were issued.

Saddle. Most cavalrymen used the 1859 McClellan saddle, which was designed by General George B. McClellan. It featured an open seat covered with rawhide, wooden stirrups, a girth strap of wool yarn, and a thick harness-leather skirt. Basic accessories included saddlebags, a currycomb, a picket pin, a lariat, a nose bag, and a "thimble" to hold the rider's carbine muzzle.

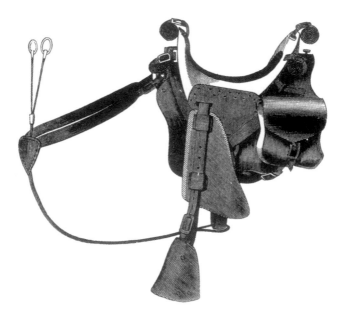

General George B. McClellan, commander of the Army of the Potomac at Antietam, created a saddle before the war that was adopted by the Union army. The McClellan saddle, complete with equipment, is pictured. (NA)

Spurs. For mounted officers, the spurs were often gilded. Enlisted men were issued spurs of brass.

HOUSEWIVES. Soldiers on both sides mended their own clothes. Most carried a "housewife," a kit containing the necessary needles, yarn, thread, and thimble, which was furnished by some mother, sister, sweetheart, or Soldier's Aid Society.

Soldiers often put off mending their clothes or darning their socks until they could either draw replacements or "find" the needed articles among belongings that a careless soldier had left unguarded for a few moments.

Some soldiers were furnished with homemade socks that had been knit, perhaps, by the women at home. Such socks usually wore well. But the men did not attempt to repair government-issue socks, which were of shoddy material and not worth the effort.

Housewives came in a variety of shapes and sizes. A typical housewife was made of cloth, with compartments for buttons and rolls of thread and a pocket to hold pins and needles. One housewife, now in a museum, was 3 inches square, made of brown leather trimmed with blue cloth and tied with blue cloth tape.

I

INSIGNIA, CONFEDERATE. An officer's rank was denoted by gold braid that encircled the cuff of his tunic. One braid indicated the rank of lieutenant; two, captain; three, field officer; and four, general officer.

On the tunic collar, rank was distinguished as follows: A general officer had wreath of gold braid enclosing three stars for a general, two for a major general, and one for a brigadier general. A colonel had three stars but not the wreath; a lieutenant colonel, two stars; and a major, one star. A captain had three horizontal bars, embroidered in gold; a first lieutenant, two bars; and a second lieutenant, one bar. Many exceptions were made late in the war because of the lack of materials.

INSIGNIA, FEDERAL. Various insignia were worn in the Union army.

Branch-of-Service Insignia. For both enlisted men and officers, branch of service was indicated by insignia on the cap or hat, trimming on the coat, and piping on the trousers. The colors were scarlet for artillery, yellow for

In the Union army, special insignia also denoted the branch of service of the wearer. Top row: infantry, ordnance, and engineers. Bottom row: artillery and cavalry. (NA)

Commodore William D. Porter, a sea dog if there ever was one, looks a bit uncomfortable on dry land. As a commodore, he has seven strips on his cuff; a rear admiral would have eight. He is wearing a cap and its device, a silver foul anchor enclosed by an oak wreath, denoting his rank. On dress occasions, he would wear a cocked hat, in the tropics a straw hat. (NA)

cavalry and engineers, sky blue for infantry, red for ordnance, and green for various rifle units.

The cap or hat insignia were crossed cannons for artillery, crossed sabers for cavalry, a turreted castle for engineers, a hunting horn for infantry, a bursting bomb for ordnance, crossed flags for signal corps, and a shield with the letters "T.E." for topographical engineers.

Enlisted men also wore their regimental numbers and company badges on their headgear. After 1863, corps badges tended to displace other insignia on caps and hats.

Officer's Insignia. Officers also wore insignia on their shoulder straps. A lieutenant general wore three silver stars; a major general, two; a brigadier general, one star; a colonel, a silver eagle; a lieutenant colonel, a silver maple leaf; a major, a gold maple leaf; a captain, two silver bars; a first lieutenant, one silver bar; and a second lieutenant and a brevet second lieutenant, nothing.

Regimental Insignia. Some regiments wore distinctive insignia of their own. Corcoran's Regiment of Irish soldiers in Meagher's Irish Brigade is a case in point. They wore a badge in the shape of an Irish Harp.

State Coat of Arms. Each state had its own coat of arms, which was prominently displayed on battle flags, belt buckles, cartridge-box plates, and especially buttons.

U.S. Coat of Arms. Army regulations defined the "Arms of the United States" as follows: "Paleways of thirteen pieces, argent and gules; a chief, azure; the escutcheon on the breast of the American eagle displayed, proper, holding in his dexter talon an olive branch, and in his left claw a bundle of thirteen arrows, all proper; and in his beak a scroll, inscribed with the motto: 'E. Pluribus Unum.' For the crest: over the head of the eagle, which appears above the escutcheon, a glory breaking through a cloud, proper and surrounding thirteen stars, forming a constellation, argent, and on an azure field."

Infantry regimental colors carried the arms of the United States, and the eagle motif was commonly used as decoration for various items of military equipment, such as drums.

K

KNAPSACKS, CONFEDERATE. Early in the war, Confederate soldiers were issued frame knapsacks similar to those of Federal soldiers. Those who came later had to make do. Some lucky rebels had knapsacks imported from Europe or captured from the Union. Others used homemade cloth satchels. Many Confederate soldiers sent their nonessentials home and wrapped their necessities in a blanket, tied the ends together, covered the blanket with a poncho, and slung it over one shoulder.

KNAPSACKS, FEDERAL. Each Union soldier was issued a knapsack to wear on his back. Knapsacks were made of painted canvas, often with the soldier's company letter and regimental number stenciled on the back.

When a knapsack was strapped on a soldier's back, his clothing was closely bound around his chest and shoulders—a painful condition for hard marching in hot weather. In addition, many of the knapsacks issued early in the war had wooden frames, and the top boards pressed directly on the shoulder blades. Rubberized knapsacks kept moisture out but were even more uncomfortable under a hot sun.

In the field, a soldier carried 45 pounds of equipment, ammunition, and rations. This included the knapsack, the haversack, a change of underclothing, an overcoat or a blanket, arms and accouterments, and half a shelter tent, as well as 40 rounds of ammunition in the soldier's cartridge box, 20 rounds in his pockets, and eight days' short rations. Under light-marching orders, the knapsack, if carried, had little more in it than a rolled blanket, extra rations, and 20 rounds of ammunition.

Late in the war, some knapsacks were replaced by Mann accouterments, which held a soldier's equipment in a suspender arrangement that kept the weight of the equipment off the soldier's loins and kidneys.

Inventors tried a number of ingenious ways to make the knapsack less burdensome. This explains the wide variety of knapsacks and knapsack accessories seen in museums and collections today.

Bondy Knapsack. This version was designed with stretchers, instead of frames, to properly position the knapsack on the back and draw it close to the shoulders.

Buchanan Knapsack. This was a knapsack of ordinary shape but equipped with yokes for the shoulders.

Clark Knapsack. To the lower side of this knapsack, a strap was buckled that passed up the front side and then split into two sections, which passed to the upper edge, where they ran over guides and from there over the shoulders and across the chest.

Griffiths Knapsack. This knapsack had an inner frame capable of being removed and folded into compact form, which permitted the knapsack to be rolled up.

Joubert Knapsack. This version combined all the parts necessary to make a litter and a shelf half, while keeping the size and weight of the knapsack equivalent to issue knapsacks.

Knapsack Collar. This heavy leather piece, which attached to the upper edge of a knapsack, fitted closely around the neck, with ends extending down in front to which straps could be attached.

Knapsack Sling. This was developed to make carrying a knapsack more comfortable. Metal slings, with a back strap below and yielding straps or loops above, could be adjusted to the shape and size of a soldier's shoulders.

Rush Knapsack. The frame of this knapsack was made of two parts hinged together. At the thick end of one part were pivoted two arms, which when extended rested on the edge of the knapsack and served to hold the canvas for forming a bed.

Short Knapsack. The unique aspect of this knapsack was the arrangement of the straps, which permitted the top of the knapsack to fall away from contact with the shoulders and spine of the wearer, allowing ventilation of the shoulders and back. In 1862, Short patented a second knapsack that featured a strap arrangement connected with a neck band, or yoke, and "steady pins" at the bottom of the knapsack to prevent it from swaying sideways.

Southward Knapsack. This knapsack was devised so that it could be adapted as a litter, a bed, a hammock, or a shelter tent, all without increasing its bulk or weight.

Sues Knapsack. The wearer could vary the position of this knapsack by using a pair of suspending straps attached to the top and the ends of the knapsack.

Sweeney and Hooten Knapsack. This version was designed to prevent the knapsack from coming into immediate contact with the back, thus minimizing heat and fatigue.

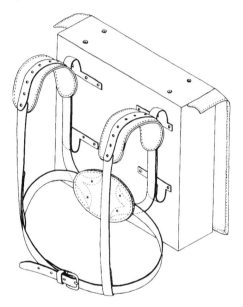

The regulation army knapsack, filled for field duty, was uncomfortable to carry on a soldier's back, caused him to sweat excessively on hot days, and had straps that often wore his skin raw. A number of inventors came up with designs to solve these problems. Shown is the Sweeney and Hooten knapsack, designed to prevent it from coming in contact with the soldier's back. (NA)

Weber, Wharton, and Snyder Knapsack. A light metal frame covered with waterproof material enabled this knapsack to be changed into a couch.

Wood's Knapsack. A system of straps, rings, and hooks allowed the soldier's musket to be attached to this knapsack. A later patent was awarded to the company for a knapsack that used hooked straps to keep it from coming in contact with the soldier's back.

KNIVES, BOWIE. Early in the war, many soldiers on both sides carried bowie knives, most being going-to-war presents from the folks at home. Northern troops generally carried English-made knives, while Confederates usually relied on homemade "bowie-type" knives.

Bowie knives were made in nearly limitless sizes and shapes. Some had 18-inch blades and weighed about 3 pounds. Very few Southern bowie knives were marked with the maker's identification.

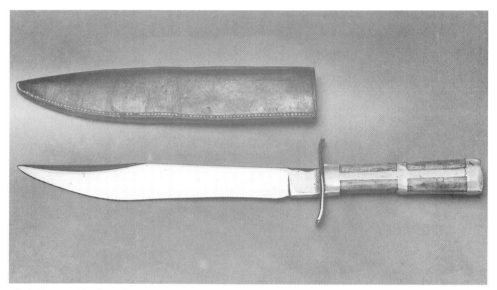

C.S. Bowie Knife. When war came, many volunteers, North and South, were presented with Bowie knives by their families or friends when they left for duty, although the knives were more apt to be used in food preparation than in combat. This knife and scabbard was taken from a Confederate prisoner at Gettysburg. (USMA)

L

LAMPS AND LANTERNS. When candles were not available, soldiers would improvise a "slush lamp," which was made by filling a sardine tin with cookhouse grease and inserting a piece of rag in one corner for a wick. The makeshift lamp was then suspended by a piece of baling wire from the ridgepole of the hut or tent. The most common lamps used candles or kerosene oil. Many of both were purchased by soldiers from sutlers or on the open market.

LANCES. Collectors sometimes confuse the lance, a steel-topped spear, with the pike, which is a wooden pole with a pointed steel head, or even the guidon pole. The lance was a little-used cavalry weapon in the Civil War, and only a few units carried them.

Some Confederate generals favored the lance because, as one explained, "the lance can be made by any carpenter and ordinary blacksmith, and is more effective than the saber."

On the Union side, several foreign soldiers of fortune attempted to raise lancer regiments. Colonel Arthur Rankin, a Canadian, recruited eight companies for a regiment, the 1st United States Lancers, but the regiment never received lances and functioned as a regular cavalry unit, armed with sabers, carbines, and revolvers.

One Federal regiment, the 6th Pennsylvania Cavalry, carried lances and used them occasionally in combat until 1863. The regiment, known as Rush's Lances, carried a lance about 9 feet long topped with a three-edged blade. The people of Philadelphia purchased 1,000 scarlet swallow-tailed pennons for the lances, and the regiment became a great favorite of artists and photographers.

M

MANUALS. Collectors prize the volumes of U.S. army training literature and regulations that were published by many commercial concerns in large Northern cities. Among these texts are the famous *Infantry Tactics* by General Winfield Scott, which consisted of three volumes that sold for $2.50 each, and *The Artillerist's Manual* by Captain John Gibbon, which sold for $5. Harper and Brothers, of New York, published the *Army Regulations*.

Official army manuals generally were issued in these quantities to each infantry regiment: 35 on army regulations, 35 on tactics, 30 on bayonet exercise, 30 on target practice, and 30 on outpost duty. Most Confederate manuals were copies of U. S. ones, with title page changes.

The following manuals also were commonly used during the war: *Army Officers' Pocket Companion* by William P. Craighill, *Gilham's Manual* by William Gilham, *Treatise on the Camp and March* by Henry D. Grafton, *A System of Target Practice* by Henry Heth, *Customs of the Service* by August V. Kautz, *Advanced-Guard, Out-Post and Detachment Service of Troops* by D. H. Mahan, *Manual of Bayonet Exercise* by George B. McClellan, *Military Dictionary* by H. L. Scott, *Manual for Engineer Troops* by J. C. Duane, *Treatise on Field Fortifications* by D. H. Mahan, *Camp and Outpost Duty* by David Butterfield, *Infantry Tactics* by Silas Casey, *Rifle and Light Infantry Tactics* by William Joseph Hardee, *Cavalry Tactics* by Philip St. George Cooke, *Instructions for Field Artillery* by Robert Anderson, and *Hand-Book of Artillery* by Joseph Roberts.

MAYNARD PRIMER. When a gun was cocked, this device pushed up a fresh prime. It was invented by a dentist named Maynard 20 years before the war, and the Model 1855 arms were manufactured with the intent of using this primer. However, the primer frequently failed to explode, and the army went back to percussion caps. A major complaint was that dampness rendered the Maynard primer useless. The container for Maynard primer was a japanned tin container, 2¾ inches tall and 1 inch in diameter.

Many manuals were published during the war to hone the skills of officers and enlisted men, army and navy, Union and Confederate. Most Confederate manuals were unauthorized reprints of Union manuals, with different covers. This selection is in the collection of the Civil War Library and Museum in Philadelphia. (CWL&M)

MEDICAL EQUIPMENT. The Union army used regulation hospital and ambulance equipment, while the Confederate army made do with whatever was available.

Hand Litters. The most common types of hand litters used by the Union army were the Saterlee, the Halstead, and the Schell. The variations among them are slight.

Hospital Knapsacks. On the battlefield, the regimental surgeon was accompanied by a hospital orderly who carried a small supply of anesthetics, styptics, stimulants, anodynes, and materials for dressings. He carried these in the Model 1859 hospital knapsack, which was made of light wood. Later, the wooden knapsack was replaced by one of wickerwork covered with canvas or enameled cloth.

In 1862, a modified version of the Model 1859 appeared. Its contents were packed in drawers, making them more accessible and less liable to become disarranged or broken.

Authentic Civil War medical equipment was displayed when the Sharpsburg, Maryland, Episcopal Church became a field hospital for the reenactment of the Battle of Antietam. At the actual battle on September 17, 1862, the bloodiest day of the war, Clara Barton and Walt Whitman were among the volunteers caring for the wounded. (CT)

In early 1863, the army approved a leather field case, or "companion," to be carried by the surgeon himself and used in place of the knapsack. It was supported by a strap passing over the shoulder and steadied by a waist strap.

Medicine Pannier. The hospital medicine chest and bulky hospital supplies were transported in wagons of the supply train and often were inaccessible when required. To remedy this, the Union began using the pannier to carry the most necessary medicines, dressings, and appliances.

Designed by a Dr. Squibb of Brooklyn, the pannier was a wooden box bound with iron and containing two compartments. When filled, it weighed 88 pounds. The medicines were packed in japanned tin bottles and boxes.

Medicines. Private companies and, late in the war, government establishments made the Union army's medicines. The Medical Purveying Depot at Astoria, New York, was one of the largest of the government establishments.

Regimental Surgeon's Medical Outfit. In addition to a special operating case to hold his equipment for amputations, a regimental surgeon received a general operating case that contained the following: 1 small amputating knife, 1 small catling, 3 bistouries, 1 hernia knife, 3 scalpels, 1 cataract needle, 1 tenaculum, 1 double hook, 6 assorted steel bougies, 6 assorted wax bougies, 3 silver catheters, 6 gum elastic catheters, 1 metacarpal saw, 1 trocar, 1 ball forceps, 1 gullet forceps, straight and curved scissors, 1 artery needle, 12 surgeon's needles, and 1 tourniquet.

Surgical Instrument Pocket Case. Pocket cases varied in size, depending on the kind and number of instruments they contained. Dr. Henry S. Hewitt, a brigade surgeon, devised a general case that he called a brigade, which contained in a compact and portable form a large and useful assortment of instruments for the army surgeon.

Cases often were adapted to the wishes of prominent surgeons. For example, Dr. William H. Van Buren's pocket cases were 5 inches long and 2½ inches wide and contained scalpel and sharp bistoury, scalpel and blunt bistoury, tenaculum and tenotomy knife, double catheter, silver probes, exploring needle, straight scissors, artery forceps, and silver director with spoon. Surgical needles and silver wire were in the pocket of the case.

MESS KNIVES, FORKS, AND SPOONS. Individual states, both North and South, furnished their soldiers with knives, forks, and spoons. These were made under contract, and the contracts varied widely from state to state, which resulted in a complete lack of uniformity. Typical government-issue knives and forks had wooden handles.

Patented Combinations. Among the many devices manufactured for the soldier market, one of the most useful was an ingenious combination of knife, fork, and spoon, which when not in use, could be folded up like a jackknife and carried in a soldier's pocket. Many soldiers bought these devices even if they already had cutlery. Several types were made by various manufacturers.

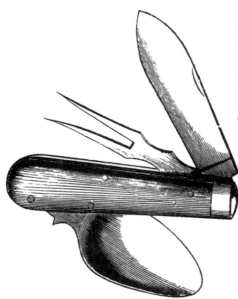

Many Federal soldiers purchased a knife-fork-spoon combination of the type shown. The handle was in two parts, joined by pins, and could be separated when used. The fork was on one half, the knife and spoon on the other. When not in use, it could be folded and carried in the soldier's pocket like a jackknife. (NA)

Cables Knife-Fork-Spoon Combination. Patented by J. J. Cables of the American Knife Co., of Plymouth Hollow, Connecticut. The two sides, when joined together, were held by headed pins on the inner scale of the fork handle, which fit into keyhole-shaped slots in the inner scale of the knife and spoon handle.

Members of the band of the 4th Michigan Infantry pose with their instruments. In the Civil War, the band always marched in front of the regiment. The unusual design of the bells of their horns sent the sound to the rear so that the soldiers could hear it more clearly. (NA)

Hardie and Hayward Knife-Fork-Spoon Combination. Patented by J. W. Hardie, of New York, and A. S. Hayward, of Boston. The handle of the knife, a single piece of metal, had a blade shaped to receive the fork and spoon handles.

Neill Knife-Fork Combination. Patented by Arthur Neill, of Boston. This combination was so constructed that either the knife or the fork could be used with the spoon.

Thorpe Knife-Fork Combination. Patented by T. B. Thorpe, of New York. This was a combined pocketknife and fork. The handle was arranged in two parts, one holding the knife and the other the fork, so that they could be disconnected and used separately.

MUSIC. Marching music was an essential ingredient of the war. It served both to lift the spirits of the men on the march and as a means of giving commands in battle. At the start of the war, Federal regiments had their own bands. Many had fife and drum corps.

Most regiments also had recreation tents or huts in which vocal or instrumental music was a feature of the evening's recreation. There were few regiments that did not have at least one violinist, one banjo player, and one bones player in its ranks. A medley of Negro and comic songs constituted the greater part of the program. A jig or clog dance might be stepped out on a hardtack box or an improvised platform.

MUSIC, SHEET. Patriotic and sentimental songs were popular on both sides with the troops at the front and the folks at home. A surprisingly large amount of sheet music from the war years has survived. Often, the songs were published with colored covers emphasizing patriotic motifs and decorated with scenes of camps and battlefields.

MUSICAL INSTRUMENTS. Most officers believed there was no better inspiration for the men at the front than a good fife and drum corps rallying upon the color line and rousing the regiment at reveille. The effect was intensified when, in a great army stretching for miles, a single bugle note gave the signal, and then from every direction came the accelerating roll of drums, the screech of fifes, and the blare of bugles and horns.

Bugle. Bugles of many types were used by both sides, but Federal bugles usually were made of copper with a brass reinforcement band around the bell. The length of a bugle usually indicates the branch of the service in which it was used. Bugles varied in length. Infantry bugles were the longest, and cavalry bugles the shortest.

Drum. Federal army drums were decorated with the U.S. coat of arms. Many authenticated drums, however, are devoid of decoration. Some drums

Appomattox Bugle. This bugle, now in the West Point Museum, sounded the last charge of General Custer's Division at Appomattox. Three types of bugles were used in the war: the cavalry bugle, the shortest at 10¼ inches, the artillery bugle (15 inches), and the infantry bugle (18½ inches). All were copper with brass trimmings. (USMA)

Two Confederate drums—which would command high prices on today's collectible market— are shown in a display of vintage musical instruments. (SB)

carried early in the war were decorated with state coats of arms, but these are extremely rare.

Fife. Most fifes were made of rosewood with silver tips, though some were made of maple with brass tips. Fifes had six small holes on one end and a larger hole on the other.

Horn. Brass wind instruments used by Civil War bands were constructed so that the bell pointed back over the musician's shoulder. The music was played for the benefit of the marching column that followed the band, not for the amusement of spectators.

Brass instruments are difficult to authenticate because no markings identified them as army band instruments and because of the popularity of brass bands in the years right after the war. All the instruments were made by private companies, which further complicates the problem.

Collectors should be aware that there were no woodwinds in Civil War bands.

MUSKETS. The musket was a smoothbore shoulder arm that fired a lead ball. Muskets were standard issue in the U.S. army until 1855, when they were replaced with a new model with a rifled bore. Although obsolete by the time of the Civil War, many muskets were in arsenals or used by militia units, both North and South, and many were used in the war. The musket was 57 inches long and weighed about 9 pounds.

Model 1855 Rifle-Musket. Called the Springfield, this was the first rifle-musket made in the United States and the first to fire the Minie ball. A shorter version, the Model 1855 rifle, had a special long-range rear sight, deadly at up to 400 yards. The rifle-musket was issued to the regular infantry and to a few elite militia units. (USMA)

Enfield Musket. One of the best and most common of the foreign arms used in the Civil War was the Model 1853 Enfield, manufactured in England. Although its caliber was a hundredth of an inch smaller than that of the Springfield, the difference did not prevent the use of the same ammunition. The Enfield was accurate to 700 yards.

Many collectors mistakenly believe that only the Confederacy used the Enfield, but the U.S. government purchased 428,000 Enfields in the early months of the war, while the Confederacy received some 400,000.

Model 1816 Musket. This was one of the oldest firearms to see extensive service in the war. It was produced from its inception until 1840 at both the Harpers Ferry and Springfield Armories, as well as by several private contractors. During that time, more than 800,000 .69-caliber Model 1816 muskets were manufactured.

Many volunteers of 1861, both Union and Confederate, found themselves armed with the 1816 percussion musket, and some Southern troops carried the flintlock. Soldiers carried these vintage arms until, either through regular issue or the fortunes of war, the guns were replaced with more modern weapons. Few Model 1816 muskets remained in active service after 1863.

Model 1842 "Springfield" Musket. The .69-caliber Model 1842 was the first U.S. musket to use the percussion-cap ignition system. From 1844 to 1855, the Harpers Ferry and Springfield Armories made some 250,000 Model 1842s. The Model 1842 was the standard long gun of the U.S. infantry before 1855.

At the outbreak of the Civil War, thousands of these arms were stored in U.S. and state arsenals, and state militias held additional thousands. As a result, the Model 1842 saw extensive action, especially in the first two years of the war. Many volunteer regiments from both the North and the South carried the Model 1842 into battle at Gettysburg in 1863.

Model 1842 "Palmetto" Musket. The .69-caliber Model 1842 Palmetto musket was produced in the early 1850s by Wm. Glaze and Co., of Columbia, South Carolina. This arm was nearly an exact duplicate of the U.S. Model 1842 Springfield percussion musket. The most noticeable variation was that the barrel bands were made of brass rather than iron.

About 6,000 of these well-made weapons were produced for the state of South Carolina. The lock plates on these muskets clearly showed their Southern heritage. Forward of the hammer was a neatly stamped palmetto tree symbol surrounded by the words "Palmetto Armory, S.C." To the rear of the hammer was stamped "Columbia, S.C." and the date. In 1861, most, if not all, of the Palmetto muskets were in the hands of the South Carolina militia, among the first troops to volunteer for the Confederacy. When they left for war, the Palmetto muskets went with them.

Collectors should beware of forged Palmetto muskets.

Remington Conversion of Model 1816 Musket. In 1855, the Remington Arms Company modernized 20,000 Model 1816 muskets by replacing the flintlock and converting the barrel breech to a percussion ignition system. The lock selected was a Remington-made model of the Maynard primer. The work was completed by 1858, and these conversions were issued to early volunteers.

P

PERCUSSION CAPS. All muskets, rifle-muskets, and rifled muskets used in the war (with a few exceptions such as the Spencer and the Henry) fired with either percussion caps or the Maynard primer. Percussion caps were carried in the cap box on the soldier's belt. Twelve caps were issued for every 10 cartridges. Loading was slow with these small caps, as they were easily dropped while being placed on the nipple of the gun.

The percussion cap for small arms was made of copper, was slightly conical with a rim at the open end, and had four slits that extended about half its height. The cap was charged with fulminate of mercury, mixed with half its weight with niter, which made the fulminate less explosive and gave body to the flame. To protect the percussion powder from moisture and to help prevent it from falling out, the cap was covered with a drop of pure shellac varnish.

PHOTOGRAPHS. The Civil War was the first American conflict to be photographed extensively. Matthew Brady, Alexander Gardner, Timothy O'Sullivan, and others followed the Union troops and sent back pictures that showed the public all aspects of the war. They captured the pageantry of the war, its horror, and the faces of the participants.

Thousands of professional photographers around the country took pictures of boys in their uniforms before they left for the war. Many of these photographs that have survived are labeled with the names of their subjects, but many more are unmarked. Many collectors today specialize in these portraits. Photos commanding premium prices include outdoor scenes, pictures of specific units, and photographs of people who are identifiable.

Ambrotype. This photographic process was invented by James Ambrose Cutting, of Boston, and his partner, Isaac Rehm, of Philadelphia. It produced a photographic image on glass, which was then backed by black paper, velvet, or even paint to make the image stand out.

The Civil War equivalent of today's Polaroid camera was the Bubroni, a combination camera and darkroom device. Chemicals sensitized the glass plate and processed it immediately after exposure. (GG)

Ambrotypes were simpler and cheaper to make than daguerreotypes, and they didn't have the double reflection that plagued the daguerreotype. Their popularity spread throughout the country. They were made in the same sizes as daguerreotypes and were sold with the same mats, preserves, and cases as daguerreotypes, which accounts for the confusion between the two.

Carte de Visite. As the name suggests, the carte de visite was inspired by the visiting card. The individual's photograph appeared on the card instead of his or her name. Cartes de visite first appeared in the 1858 Exhibition of the Franklin Institute in Philadelphia, and from 1860 to 1866, the fad spread like

Officers in the war gave their photographic portraits to their families and friends. As a rule, the higher the rank of the officer, the more portraits he distributed. A major general might dispense thousands. Many such portraits found their way into the card photo albums that were popular in the 1860s. (GG)

wildfire throughout the country. An album was marketed for storing and preserving the cards in the home.

Daguerreotype. A daguerreotype was a photograph produced on a silver or a silver-covered copper plate. The first process to popularize photography, daguerreotype was invented by Frenchman Louis J. M. Daguerre in 1839. During the 1840s and '50s, "daguerreotype salons" were established in many American cities.

During the war, daguerreotypes were sold in attractive cases that were embossed with decorative designs, including military symbols such as crossed cannons and the American flag. Daguerreotypes were costly and not as popular with the common soldier as either ambrotypes or tintypes.

Daguerreotypes were made in various sizes. The most common was the $1/6$ size, the silver plate of which measured 2¾ by 3¼ inches. Since daguerreotypes were direct pictures, the image was reversed, as in the case of a person seeing himself in a mirror.

A simple test distinguishes a daguerreotype. Hold the photograph in your hand and move it through various angles. If the photographic image can be seen clearly in some positions and only shiny metal in others, it is a daguerreotype.

Daguerreotypes can be restored to nearly original condition, but it is job for a specialist, and only a few laboratories are competent to do such work. A finger should never touch the surface of a daguerreotype. This could destroy the image, with no chance for restoration.

Tintype. Hamilton L. Smith, a professor at Kenyon College in Ohio, patented a process for making "photographic pictures on japanned surfaces." Tintypes were also known as melanotypes and ferrotypes, but most people called them tintypes and the name stuck.

At first, tintypes were made in similar sizes and placed in similar cases as daguerreotypes and ambrotypes. But producing tintypes became so inexpensive that photographers went after customers who would spend only a dollar or less to have their pictures taken. Some tintypes were no larger than postage stamps and were placed in simple paper mats.

After a larger tintype had been mounted in a case, it was difficult to distin-

Cameras of the Civil War era used huge lenses, particularly when compared with a tiny modern camera. Vintage lenses did not have diaphragms to control the light passing through them and instead used metal slides, like the one in the foreground, which were inserted in a slot on the side of the lens. (GG)

guish from an ambrotype. To make a proper identification, remove the photograph from the case. If the picture is on metal, it is a tintype; if on glass, an ambrotype.

Stereoscopic View. Another photographic fad was collecting three-dimensional stereoscopic views of the war. One of the main producers of these was the E. and H. T. Anthony Co., of New York. In the April 15, 1865, *Army and Navy Journal,* the company advertised stereoscopic views "obtained at great expense and forming a complete Photographic History of the Great Union Contest." Among the views mentioned were those of Bull Run, Yorktown, Hanover Junction, and Fort Morgan.

Many European images have been misrepresented as images of the Civil War. Collectors should also beware of images of reenactors that have been put in old frames and offered as originals.

Stereoscopic Viewer.

PIKES. Used only a few times in the war, pikes were secondary arms made to relieve the shortage of arms in the Confederacy. John Brown and his gang carried pikes when they attempted to seize the Union armory at Harpers Ferry. One Confederate artillery unit used pikes during the Seven Days' Battles around Richmond.

Most pikes were locally manufactured weapons for Confederate use. The first ones were made by Ross Winns, of Baltimore, but most were made in Georgia to be used against General William T. Sherman's troops. One maker of Georgia pikes was Samuel Griswold, who turned out a clover-leaf type.

Although it looks like a secret weapon, this is a four-tube camera, which can expose four images on a single plate. Used by photographers who went from army camp to army camp taking portraits of soldiers, it speeded up the process and lowered the cost of making the photographs. (GG)

Captain Franz Reuter, of Louisiana, invented a pike consisting of a scythe blade on a 10-foot pole. Some pikes built in Alabama had a keen two-edged steel head like a bowie knife.

POSTERS AND BROADSIDES. Civil War posters and broadsides are of an almost endless variety and constitute a complete collecting field. Most were appeals for enlistment that were posted in prominent places and directed the local citizenry to join a specific unit being raised in their locality. Such posters were usually printed in small numbers and used only for a few weeks. As a result, posters and broadsides are quite rare.

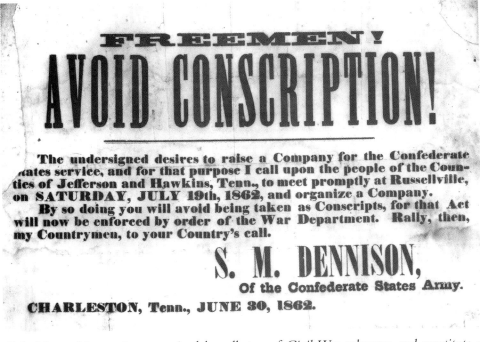

Colorful recruiting posters are prized by collectors of Civil War ephemera and constitute a collecting field in itself. Posters are rare, and the variety is almost limitless. Placed in prominent places, they were directed to the local citizenry. Printed in small numbers, they were usually displayed for a few weeks at most. (NA)

PROJECTILES. The Union army used a variety of projectiles in its artillery weapons.

Bar Shot. This projectile was like chain shot, except a bar of iron connected its two round shot.

Case Shot. This shot consisted of small balls enclosed in a case that, when broken by the shock of the discharge in the piece or by a charge of powder within the case, exploded during flight, scattering the balls. The kinds of case shot used in the war included canister shot, grapeshot, and spherical case shot.

Canister Shot. Canister shot turned cannons into giant shotguns, firing a number of murderous metal pellets rather than a single shell. Most destructive at 100 to 200 yards, canister was limited to ranges not exceeding 400 yards. Canister shot used cylindrical tin cases with iron heads, filled with cast-iron balls arranged in four tiers and packed with dry sawdust.

Grapeshot. A stand of grapeshot consisted of nine shots put together by means of two cast-iron plates, two rings, and a bolt and nut. The projectile was attached by tin straps to a wooden sabot, to which was also attached the cartridge bag containing the charge. The Union army discontinued the use of grapeshot in 1863 because canister had proved more effective and was easier to fabricate. The navy probably continued to use old pattern grapeshot, often called quilted grapeshot, throughout the war.

Spherical Case Shot. This shot consisted of a thin shell of cast iron containing a number of musket balls and a charge of powder sufficient to burst the shell. As in an ordinary shell, a fuse was fixed to it to ignite the charge.

Chain Shot. This was two round shot held together by a chain. Their motion of rotation would have made these projectiles valuable in cutting masts and riggings of ships if their flight had not been so inaccurate.

Fire Ball. This was an oval projectile formed of sacks of canvas filled with a combustible composition that emitted a bright flame. The fire ball was used to illuminate the enemy's works and was loaded with a shell.

Grenade. A grenade was a shell thrown by hand or by large-caliber mortars and ignited by means of a fuse. The two main types were hand grenades and rampart grenades. Grenades were useful in defending works. Small grenades could be thrown by hand into trenches, into covered approaches, or at besiegers mounting a breach. Large grenades could be rolled over the parapet or propelled by mortars.

Light Ball. This was similar to the fire ball, except it did not contain a shell. It was used to light up one's own works.

Shell. A shell was a hollow sphere of cast iron containing powder that was ignited by means of a fuse. When fired at troops, the shell was prepared so that it would explode over their heads or, if the terrain was suitable for ricochets, in front of the enemy. When fired at works or buildings, the shell exploded after penetration.

Smoke Ball. This was a hollow paper sphere similar to the light ball, but filled with a composition that emitted a dense, nauseating smoke. The smoke ball was used to conceal one's own operations. The smoke ball burned 25 to 30 minutes.

Solid Shot. This solid sphere of cast iron was used almost exclusively in guns. The gun itself usually derived its denomination from the weight of the shot, as in 6-pounder or 12-pounder.

The Confederate artillery used various types of projectiles and fuses, including imported ones. They also used copies and adaptations of Federal projectiles.

The mammoth weapon on the railroad flatcar is the 13-pound Union mortar "Dictator," which pounded Confederate positions relentlessly at Petersburg. Mortars, whatever their size, are ideal siege weapons because they can lob shells sufficiently high to clear the earthworks and land in the area occupied by enemy troops. (LC)

R

REVOLVERS. A revolver is a handgun with a cylinder containing several chambers. Cocking the hammer brings the chambers successively in line with the barrel. When the trigger is pulled, the hammer falls and discharges the bullet in the chamber.

Adams Revolver. A high-quality, double-action, five-shot percussion revolver, the Adams was a British arm that was also manufactured by the Massachusetts Armory Company, of Chicopee. Private arms dealers imported Adams revolvers, and they were carried by some officers in both the Union and Confederate armies.

Adams Revolver. Collectors prize the rare Adams, a high-quality British double-action revolver that was also manufactured in the United States. The Union army bought about 600 but did not adopt them for wartime use. However, a number of Union and Confederate soldiers carried their own into battle. (USMA)

Colt Model 1851 Navy and Model 1860 Army Revolvers. These revolvers, the most famous and widely used in the Civil War, were known as reliable, effective weapons even before the war began. They were manufactured by the Colt Firearms Company, of Hartford. Union officers preferred Colts as their private side arms. Colts accounted for 38 percent of the total revolvers purchased for the Union army, and most went to arm cavalrymen. Confederate volunteers often went to war carrying these Colt revolvers.

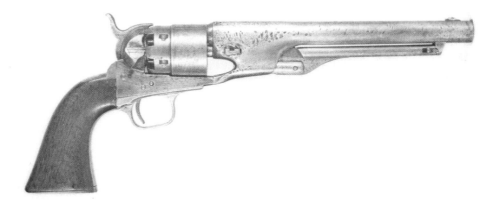

Colt Model 1860 Army Revolver. The most widely used Union revolver was the Colt. The dependable Colt was a popular handgun before the war, and many Confederates carried Colts they had purchased before the war. Nearly 4 out of 10 revolvers purchased by the Union army were Colts, and they were used in every battle in the war. (USMA)

Confederate "Colt" Revolvers. Among the rarest Civil War pistols in collections today are the Confederate copies of prewar Colt revolvers. Seven different arms makers produced these much-needed weapons for the Confederacy. The largest producer was the firm of Griswold and Gunnison, of Griswoldville, Georgia. Its revolvers had a distinctive brass frame mounted with a steel cylinder and barrel.

Most Confederate "Colts" were copies of the .44-caliber 1860 Colt Army revolver. The copies were reliable and well made, but none achieved the quality and finish of the originals.

Kerr Revolver. Manufactured by the London Armory Company, the

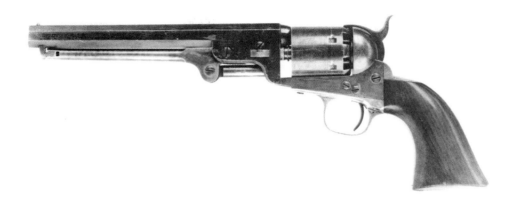

Colt Model 1851 Navy Revolver. The terms Army *and* Navy *did not refer to the branch of the armed service to which the model was supplied, but to its caliber. Army revolvers were .44 caliber; Navy examples were .36s. Collectors prize Civil War Colts, and many consider the Colt Navy to be the most beautiful handgun ever made. (USMA)*

Kerr revolver was one of the more interesting weapons imported by the Confederacy. A five-shot percussion revolver that could be fired either single- or double-action, the Kerr was a well-made, serviceable weapon, equal in quality to any used in the war. Confederate cavalrymen carried more Kerr revolvers than they did all other handguns combined.

Lefaucheux Revolver. This French revolver was one of the few handguns imported by the U.S. government. Some 12,000 were purchased and used mostly to arm troops serving in the western theater. Significantly, the Lefaucheux was the only nonpercussion handgun purchased by either side.

The Lefaucheux was the first handgun issued that used internally primed ammunition. It required a unique pin-fire cartridge that was difficult to manufacture. The Confederacy purchased few, if any, Lefaucheux revolvers, although some Southern officers carried them. Confederate General Stonewall Jackson's men presented him with an elaborately engraved Lefaucheux.

LeMat Revolver. The most exotic and formidable handgun used in the war was the .40-caliber LeMat, a single-action percussion revolver with a nine-shot cylinder. The cylinder revolved around a separate, .63-caliber smooth-bore barrel that extended forward under the conventional, .40-caliber rifled

Kerr Revolver. The Confederacy relied heavily on imported handguns, and the five-shot, .44-caliber English-made Kerr proved to be one of the best. It carried five shots and could be fired either single- or double-action. More Kerrs were carried by Confederate cavalrymen than all the Confederate-made guns combined. (USMA)

LeMat Revolver. This was the most powerful handgun of the war, firing either .40-caliber bullets or 16-gauge shotgun shells. The LeMat is also one of the rarest. None were used by the Union army. The Confederacy imported only 1,500, and the LeMat was carried by General J. E. B. Stuart and other high-ranking officers. (USMA)

barrel. The smoothbore barrel was loaded with buckshot and fired separately. The hammer was fitted with a pivoting head that, when flipped down, redirected the strike to fire the shotgun barrel. For close combat, the LeMat was unequaled by any revolver of its time.

Although the inventor lived in New Orleans, the LeMat was made in both Paris and London. The Confederacy imported some 1,500. The famous cavalry leader J. E. B. Stuart carried a LeMat, as did several other Southern generals.

Remington Model 1861 Army and Model 1862 Navy Revolvers. Remington revolvers, in both .44 and .36 calibers, were second only to Colts in the number that saw service. Remingtons accounted for nearly 35 percent of the revolvers purchased by the U.S. government.

Savage Navy Revolver. The Savage's unusually large trigger guard, containing two triggers, made it one of the most distinctive-looking revolvers used in the war. One trigger, ending in a finger-size ring, actually was a lever that, when pulled, rotated the cylinder and cocked the hammer.

The Union purchased some 12,000 Savages, issuing most of them to cavalry in the western theater. Many also were privately purchased and smuggled South, and some Confederate cavalrymen carried Savages.

The Savage Navy was a single-action, six-shot percussion revolver. But the odd construction of this revolver made it poorly balanced and difficult to aim, and it was not a popular weapon.

Spiller and Burr Revolver. This was the only revolver manufactured in quantity in the Confederacy that was not a copy of a Colt. After production difficulties caused the abandonment of the Colt design, the Spiller and Burr was substituted. It was a .36-caliber revolver with a cast-brass frame and a steel barrel and cylinder. It followed the pattern of the all-steel, U.S.-made Whitney Navy revolver. Some 1,400 Spiller and Burr revolvers were produced from 1862 to 1864.

Starr Army Revolver. This was the only American revolver produced during the war in both single- and double-action models. Most of the revolvers manufactured by the Starr Arms Company, of Yonkers, New York, were purchased by the U.S. government for issue to the cavalry. All were six-shot

Leech & Rigdon Revolver. Considered the best of the Confederate-made copies of the Colts, this .36-caliber revolver had a dragoon-type iron barrel and an iron frame with brass back straps and trigger guard. Some 1,500 of these six-shot pistols were produced. (USMA)

Starr Army Revolver. Starr Army handguns were the only American revolvers produced during the war in both single- and double-action models. The single-action model, pictured, was supplied to the Union cavalry. Although the double-action model was the more modern, the single-action was cheaper to produce. (USMA)

percussion revolvers. While the double-action Starr was easier to fire, the single-action was cheaper to produce.

Whitney Navy Revolver. The Whitney, manufactured by the Whitney Arms Company, of New Haven, was a six-shot, single-action percussion revolver. Of the some 30,000 of these revolvers produced during the war, half were purchased by the U.S. government and issued to volunteer cavalry troops. Many were purchased privately by Union officers, who considered the Whitney a well-made and very serviceable side arm.

Whitney Navy Revolver. A well-made and serviceable .36-caliber, six-shot revolver, the Whitney was issued to volunteer cavalry units, and many Union officers purchased them for their own use. Some 30,000 were manufactured during the war. The example shown is engraved with the battles in which its owner saw action. (USMA)

RIFLE-MUSKETS. The rifle-musket was a shoulder arm about 56 inches long that was manufactured with a rifled bore. The United States adopted its first rifle-musket in 1855, and the arm quickly replaced the common musket as standard issue. More common in the North than in the South, the rifle-musket had a high degree of accuracy.

Austrian Lorenz Rifle-Musket. The Model 1865 rifle-musket, known as the Lorenz, was the most widely used of several types of muskets imported from Austria. Second only to the British Pattern '53 Enfield in imports, the Lorenz saw service in both theaters of the war. It was imported in several calibers, but the most popular and most commonly used was the .54 caliber.

There was a heavy concentration of these arms in the Confederate Army units in the western theater. Both North and South imported the Lorenz throughout the war.

British Pattern '53 Enfield Rifle–Musket. The Enfield was the second most widely used infantry weapon of the war. It was imported in large quantities by both North and South and saw service in every major battle from early 1862 on.

The Pattern '53 was the standard arm of the British army from 1853 to 1867. Originally produced for British service at the Royal Small Arms Factory in Enfield, England, was well made and deadly accurate. From an American standpoint, an important consideration was its .577 caliber, which allowed the use of ammunition made for the .58-caliber arms that were standard in both the Union and Confederate armies.

C.S. Richmond Rifle–Musket. Like the C.S. Richmond rifle, this Confederate-made rifle-musket was produced with machinery captured at the Federal armory at Harpers Ferry in 1861. It was a close copy of the U.S. Model 1855/61 rifle-musket, but bearing the same distinct differences as the C.S. Richmond rifle.

Model 1842 Rifle–Musket. In 1855, the Federal government returned its Model 1842 smoothbore muskets to its arsenals to have the barrels rifled. The original Model 1842 had no rear sight. The additional range and accuracy gained by rifling made a rear sight desirable, and many were added by armories and private contractors.

Model 1855 Rifle–Musket. This was the first real rifle-musket produced by the United States. It was manufactured at both government armories, Springfield and Harpers Ferry. The Model 1855 was also the first U.S. firearm to fire a new bullet-shaped projectile—the famed .58-caliber Minie ball.

A distinctive feature of the weapon was its lock, which contained the Maynard primer system. This eliminated the need for a percussion cap by substituting a roll of caps, similar to those used in 20th-century toy cap pistols. By cocking the hammer, the soldier fed a cap out and over the nipple. When he pulled the trigger, the cap was forced onto the nipple, and the resulting explosion fired the arm.

Although a few elite militia units were armed with the 1855 rifle-musket, this weapon was primarily the firearm of the regular infantry. When Confederate forces seized the Harpers Ferry Armory in 1861, they made off with the machinery used to produce the Model 1855.

Model 1861 Rifle-Musket. This was the classic arm of the Civil War infantry soldier, the standard against which all other wartime shoulder arms were judged. It was a refinement of the first U.S. rifle-musket, the Model 1855, but the Maynard primer and the patch box were eliminated, which simplified the arm without diminishing its quality.

The Model 1861 was originally manufactured solely at the Springfield Armory. The war emergency, however, called for far more arms than could be produced at Springfield. To meet the need, the Ordnance Department contracted with 20 separate manufacturers to produce the arm. The sole deviation was the contractor's name on the lock plate instead of that of the National Armory. More than 700,000 Model 1861 rifle-muskets were produced during the war years.

Saxon Model 1851 and Model 1857 "Dresden" Rifle-Muskets. Among the best made of the many foreign arms were the .58-caliber Models 1851 and 1857 rifle-muskets. Purchased in Dresden, Germany, they were usually referred to as "Dresden rifles" by the men who carried them. The two models varied only in barrel length—the Model 1857 was 3 inches longer than the earlier model. The most distinctive feature of these weapons was their unique double middle-barrel band.

Some 27,000 Models 1851 and 1857 were imported into the United States by both the North and South early in the war. The U.S. Ordnance Department considered them first-class arms, well constructed and reliable. Numerous photographs exist of Union soldiers proudly holding their Dresdens.

Special Model 1861 and Model 1863 Rifle-Muskets. These two firearms were similar in appearance and identical in function to the Model 1861 rifle-musket, but several differences made them distinct: They did not have the small clean-out screw in the bolster immediately below the nipple, or band retaining springs; they used screw-tightened, clamp-type barrel bands.

A later version of the Model 1863 reintroduced the band retaining springs when it was found that the band screws worked loose during firing.

RIFLES. The rifle is a shoulder arm with a rifled bore. In the mid–19th century, the rifle was distinguished from the musket and the rifle-musket by its shorter barrel. The shorter length made the rifle ideal for mounted infantry troops or for skirmishers, for whom maneuverability was vital.

"American" Rifles. Individually crafted muzzle-loading target rifles were known as "American" rifles. They were precision instruments, always fitted with either telescopic or finely adjusted peep sights. These rifles were used only at the beginning of the war. Because they were individually made, the physical appearance and dimensions of "American" rifles varied greatly in length, weight, and caliber.

Near-pinpoint accuracy at ranges of up to 1,000 yards could be expected from these rifles. A target the size of an enemy soldier was an easy mark at much greater distances. Several companies and three full regiments of men were raised to serve as sharpshooters in the Union army.

Colt Revolving Rifle. This unique .56-caliber breech-loading rifle was first produced in 1855 and submitted to the U.S. army for field tests two years later. Made by the Colt Firearms Company, of Hartford, it was a greatly enlarged version of the famous Colt revolver. The revolving rifle was considered too complex for military use, but the Union army purchased and issued some 4,600 of them. After the war, the few Colt revolving rifles remaining in service were sold as surplus for as little as 40 cents each.

C.S. Richmond Rifle. The C.S. Richmond rifle and rifle-musket were produced in larger quantities than any other Confederate-made shoulder arm. These well-made muzzleloaders were close copies of the U.S. Model 1855 rifle and Model 1855/1861 rifle-musket.

Compared with their Yankee counterparts, the Richmond Rifles had several distinct differences. Most noticeable was the plain "humpback" lock plate. To facilitate manufacture, the Confederates immediately eliminated the Maynard primer system found on the Model 1855 Harpers Ferry arms. Using the Harpers Ferry dies, they produced a lock with the outline of the Model

1855 lock but without the milling required for the Maynard primer. This distinctive lock was then stamped "C.S." over "Richmond, Va." forward of the hammer, with the date of manufacture to the rear. These rifles were often referred to as "Confederate Springfields," a term that attested not only to their appearance but also to their quality.

Fayetteville Rifle. This muzzle-loading rifle was produced in Fayetteville, North Carolina, using machinery captured at the Harpers Ferry Armory in April 1861. Production began in early 1862 and continued until the end of the war. The Fayetteville rifle resembled the U.S. Model 1855 rifle, including the barrel lug for the Model 1855 sword bayonet. A copy of that bayonet also was manufactured in Fayetteville.

As with most Confederate copies of U.S. arms, there were deviations incorporated to ease manufacture. The butt plate and nose cap on the Fayetteville rifle were of brass rather than iron. Early-production Fayettevilles had the plain "humpback" lock plate seen on C.S. Richmond arms. Forward of the hammer, the lock was stamped "Fayetteville," with an eagle over the letters "C.S.A." The date of manufacture appeared on the back of the hammer.

Henry Rifle. The Henry rifle was the most technically advanced firearm to see service in the Civil War. Patented in 1860, it was a .44-caliber, lever-action, magazine-fed breechloader, and its fire power was unequaled. At a

Henry Rifle. The best firearm of the war was the Henry rifle, a lever-action rifle that carried 15 bullets in its magazine. However, the Union Chief of Ordnance could see no advantage to the Henry over single-shot rifles. Only 1,731 were purchased, but more saw service because many soldiers willingly bought their own. (USMA)

time when muzzle-loading rifles were by far the most widely used weapons, and when single-shot breechloaders were considered modern, the Henry's 15-shot magazine offered a decided advantage.

The famed Winchester lever-action rifle, still in use today, was a direct descendent of the Henry. This was not coincidental. Although the patent for the Henry was held by its inventor, B. Tyler Henry, the rights to the patent were held by his employer, Oliver F. Winchester.

In the end, the government purchased only 1,731 Henrys, but thousands more were used in battle by soldiers who saw their value and were willing to pay $40 for one.

The only arms that came close to the Henry in technology were the Spencer rifle and carbine. The Spencer was easier to produce—a major reason that it became the dominant magazine-fed arm of the war. Despite government reluctance and competition from the Spencer arms, more than 10,000 Henry rifles had been produced by 1865.

Merrill Rifle. The .54-caliber Merrill rifle was yet another breechloader used in the war. It employed a unique top-opening loading mechanism. The shooter raised the lever and brought it back toward himself, thus exposing a chamber into which he inserted the bullet with its combustible cartridge.

When the chamber lever was closed, a small piston forced the cartridge itself forward and seated it and the bullet in the chamber. The Merrill's paper cartridge employed an external priming system, which took the form of a standard musket cap that was ignited by a lock and hammer identical to the one used in a standard musket.

Only 769 Merrill rifles were purchased by the Union army, although the Merrill was used in both theaters of the war. In the East, part of the 1st Battalion Massachusetts Sharpshooters, which helped stop Pickett's Charge at Gettysburg, was armed with them. In the West, the 21st Indiana Infantry also used the Merrill. Both units spoke highly of its accuracy.

Model 1841 "Mississippi" Rifle. This muzzleloader was one of the most famous and widely used arms of its type. The Model 1841 first gained recognition in the hands of a regiment of Mississippi volunteers in the Mexican War, hence the nickname "Mississippi" rifle. An exceptionally handsome weapon, the Model 1841 was fitted with brass barrel bands and trigger guard. Added to this was a large brass patch box set in its dark walnut stock. Originally issued in .54 caliber, many Model 1841s were rerifled to the U.S. government's standard .56 caliber after 1855. In either caliber, the Mississippi was well known for its deadly long-range accuracy.

The Mississippi was produced at the U.S. armory at Harpers Ferry and by four private contractors. Production began in 1842 and continued until 1855. During this period, more than 75,000 Model 1841 rifles were manufactured. At the outbreak of the war, the state of New York purchased 5,000 Model 1841s from the Remington Arms Company.

The Model 1841 saw extensive service in the hands of both Union and Confederate soldiers. It was a favorite arm of Confederate mounted troops, as well as of the infantry on both sides. One of the regiments engaged at Gettysburg, the 45th New York Infantry, was armed with this rifle.

Model 1841 "Palmetto" Rifle. This .54-caliber muzzle-loading rifle, manufactured from 1852 to 1853 by Wm. Glaze and Co., of Columbia, South Carolina, was an exact duplicate of the U.S. Model 1841 Mississippi rifle. Only about 1,000 Palmettos were made, and they were used to arm the South Carolina militias.

The quality and workmanship of the Palmetto rifle were equal to those of the Model 1841. The lock plate was marked with a palmetto tree encircled by the words "Palmetto Armory, S.C." forward of the hammer. To the rear of the hammer was stamped "Columbia, S.C. 1852."

Model 1855 Rifle. A shorter version of the Model 1855 rifle-musket, the Model 1855 rifle was produced at the U.S. armory at Harpers Ferry from 1857 to 1861. Many of these were fitted with a special long-range rear sight that permitted accurate fire at up to 400 yards.

Sharps Rifle. This was the best known of the breech-loading rifles, largely due to its use by the legendary 1st and 2nd Regiments of the U.S. Sharp-shooters. The Sharps was a .52-caliber, breech-loading, single-shot rifle. The shooter had to open the breech and manually insert a cartridge each time he wanted to fire. Although this method did not permit the rate of fire of such rifles as the Spencer and Henry, it was a significant improvement over the muzzle-loading method in general use during the war.

The Sharps used a combustible cartridge made of linen or paper treated with nitrate. When the rifle was fired, the cartridge was consumed by the ignition of the powder charge it contained. The cartridge was externally primed, requiring the soldier to place a standard musket percussion cap on a nipple in the rifle's breech, which was then struck by the hammer to achieve ignition.

Spencer Rifle. Next to the Henry, the Spencer rifle was the most technically advanced small arm of the war. Invented by Christopher Spencer, a former Colt Firearms employee, the Spencer was an idea whose time had come. This breechloader did not see action until early 1863, but from that point, it rewrote the history of warfare.

The Spencer rifle featured a tubular feed magazine that held seven internally primed, metallic-cased, .56-caliber cartridges. The magazine was contained in the rifle's buttstock and was itself loaded through the butt plate. By means of lever action, the rifle's ingenious mechanism first ejected the empty cartridge case from the previously fired round and then fed a fresh cartridge into the chamber. The soldier then simply had to cock the external hammer, aim, and shoot. The Spencer's rate of fire was limited only by the shooter's speed in firing.

Whitworth Rifle. This rifle resembled the British Pattern '53 Enfield rifle-musket, but that was as far as the similarity went. The British Whitworth was a .45-caliber muzzleloader with a hexagonal bore, and the unique Whitworth bullet was shaped to fit the bore. Also unique was the positioning of the telescopic sight on the left side of the stock opposite the lock plate.

With its telescopic sight, this rifle could be counted on for killing accuracy at ranges of up to 1,500 yards. Brought to Southern ports by blockade-runners, it was a favorite weapon of Confederate sharpshooters.

S

SHOULDER STRAPS, ARMY. Union army regulations stipulated that officers wear shoulder straps on their uniforms.

For commanding generals, the shoulder strap was made of dark blue cloth, measuring 1⅜ inches wide by 4 inches long; bordered with an embroidery of gold, ¼ inch wide; and with three silver-embroidered stars of five rays, a large one on the center of the strap and a smaller one on each side equidistant between the center and the outer edge of the strap.

For other major generals, the strap had two stars instead of three. Both stars were the same size, and the center of each was 1 inch from the outer edge of the gold embroidery on the ends of the strap. For brigadier generals, the strap had only one star, with the center of the star equidistant from the outer edge of the embroidery on the ends of the strap. Colonels had embroidered silver spread eagles rather than stars. The cloth of the strap varied in color: for artillery, it was scarlet; for cavalry, yellow; for general staff and staff corps, dark blue; and for infantry, light or sky blue.

An officer's shoulder straps told his rank. First column, top to bottom: lieutenant general, major general, and brigadier general. Second column, colonel, lieutenant colonel, and major. Third column, captain, first lieutenant, and second lieutenant. (NA)

Straps for majors and captains were the same as for colonels, but with gold leaves and bands rather than the eagle. On the first lieutenant's strap, the eagle was replaced with a gold-embroidered band at each end. Second lieutenants and brevet second lieutenants wore straps like those for colonels, but also with the eagle omitted.

The Confederate army did not use shoulder straps on officers' uniforms, although photographs and uniforms exist that show that some Confederate officers wore copies of Union shoulder straps.

SHOULDER STRAPS, NAVY, CONFEDERATE. The newly created Confederate navy used shoulder straps on many uniforms.

The flag officer's strap was made of sky blue cloth edged with black and bordered with an embroidery of gold. The strap had four stars. A captain's strap was the same as the flag officer's, except that it had three stars. A commander's strap had two stars, a lieutenant's had one star, and a master's strap had none.

SHOULDER STRAPS, NAVY, FEDERAL. U.S. navy shoulder straps were made of navy blue cloth embroidered in gold.

The center and end ornaments distinguished between line and staff and indicated rank: rear admiral—a silver foul anchor in the center, a silver star at each end; commodore—a silver star, embroidered on a gold foul anchor; captain—a silver spread eagle, resting on a plain anchor; commander—a silver foul anchor in the center and a silver oak leaf at each end; lieutenant-commander—the same but with gold oak leaves; lieutenant and master—a silver foul anchor, with gold bars at each end. Midshipmen, third assistant engineers, and clerks did not wear shoulder straps.

Gunners, boatswains, carpenters, and sailmakers wore shoulder straps of plain gold lace. Boatswains had the letter "B" and carpenters had the letter "C" embroidered in silver.

SIGNAL EQUIPMENT. A Federal signal officer was expected to have in his possession for immediate use a full set of signal equipment.

Canteen. The canteen was made of copper, with one seam, and had a carrying strap. It held 1 gallon of turpentine or other flammable fluid.

Cipher Disk. Made of cardboard, the cipher disk consisted of two concentric disks, one smaller than the other. Letters, phrases, and numerals around the edge of one disk corresponded with signal numbers on the

Signal Corps officers were supplied with a cipher disk like the one at right with which to encode and decode messages. On the cardboard disks were written or printed the letters of the alphabet and symbols of numbers in irregular sequence around the circumference. (NA)

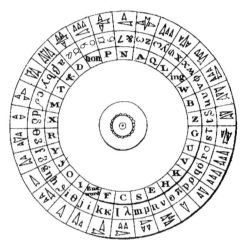

circumference of the other. Revolving the disk changed the cipher.

Compass. Officers of the Signal Corps were furnished with a good pocket compass, which was useful in conducting reconnaissance and in locating signal stations, both friendly and hostile.

Field Glass. This glass had a low magnifying power but an extensive field of view. It was used in sweeping the landscape to find the enemy's artillery, pickets, tents, wagons, and other objects, which would then be examined more closely with a telescope.

Haversack. This contained wicking, wind matches, pliers, shears for trimming the torch, a small funnel for filling the torch, two flame shades, and a wind shade.

Kit. This canvas case contained the signal flags, staff, torch case, torches, and wormer, all compactly rolled together and bound by straps.

Flags. The signal flags were made of cotton or linen. There were seven of them, as follows:

6-foot white square with a 2-foot red square at the center

6-foot black square with a 2-foot white square at the center

4-foot white square with a 16-inch red square at the center

4-foot black square with a 16-inch white square at the center

4-foot red square with a 16-inch white square at the center

2-foot white square with an 8-inch red square at the center

2-foot red square with an 8-inch white square at the center

All of these flags were fitted with tapes for tying them to the staff.

Staff. The signal staff was made of hickory and had four ferruled joints. The fourth joint was the one to which the flag was attached for day signals.

Torch Case. The torch case was a piece of rubber cloth, and was fitted on one side with pouches into which the torches were inserted.

Torches. Torches could be read by night from distances of 8 to 25 miles, depending upon conditions. It was an 18-inch copper cylinder that was closed at the lower end, except for a nozzle through which the torch was filled.

Wormer. This was a screw used when the torch wick was accidentally drawn so far into the tube of the torch that it could not be seized by pliers.

SIGNAL PISTOLS. The Federal signal pistol resembled a handgun with the barrel removed. Both the army and navy used "Composition Fires" cartridges in their signal pistols. These were pyrotechnic compositions that burned with a great intensity of light and color. They were fired by the explosion of the percussion cap on the pistol.

Signal colors were indicated by matching colors on the cartridge cases. There were 10 different colors, although red, white, and green were used most often. Generally, message signals consisted of two colored lights. For example, white and red might mean the enemy was approaching, while white and white might mean the enemy was retreating.

SIGNAL ROCKETS. These rockets were paper or pasteboard cylinders filled with charges. Usually, a quick-match fuse was used. A yard of quick-match burned for 12 seconds, so ignition of the rockets could be set by using the appropriate length of fuse. Signal rockets were fired from a frame.

Signal rockets attained great elevation and generally could be seen up to 8 miles. They were not particularly successful in wooded terrain because observers usually had to be above the trees to see the rockets properly. When clouds hung low, rockets threw out their stars above the clouds and could not be seen.

SIGNAL TELESCOPE. The Federal Signal Corps telescope was considered to be the best in general use at the time. This telescope was 30-power and had a focal length of 26 inches. The tube was cased in leather. The draw was of four joints, bronzed black so that there would be no glitter to attract the enemy. It had leather caps for both ends and a strong leather carrying strap.

STENCILS. Many military units required that items of equipment and clothing be stenciled with the owner's name. Such markings sometimes included the soldier's company and regiment numbers. Individual soldiers, both North and South, often had their own stencils, usually made of brass, indicating their names, companies, and regiments. Stenciling often served to identify a soldier if he became a casualty.

STOVES, CAMP. While the Sibley stove was the most common, a wide variety of camp stoves were used by both the North and South. The large, cumbersome types were used mainly in rear echelons or at large headquarters.

Hope Stove. This stove, manufactured in Castleton, Vermont, consisted of a box top of sheet metal, provided with holes for the chimney and a kettle. The stove was designed for use over a trench cut in the ground.

Sibley Stove. This cone-shaped stove was used in conjunction with the Sibley tent. The stovepipe was connected to the stove proper, which stood beneath the tripod supporting the tent. A chain with a hook at the end to hold a kettle hung from the fork of the tripod.

The Sibley stove was an airtight cylinder that was 30 inches tall with an 18-inch base and that weighed 30 pounds. During the war, the Union army used about 16,000 Sibley stoves. The Sibley stove was manufactured and sold until early in the 20th century.

Soyers New Field Stove. This stove was quite fuel-efficient, consuming not more than 12 to 15 pounds of fuel, which would be 300 pounds of coal per 1,000 men. Salt beef, Irish stew, stewed beef, tea, and coffee could be prepared on the Soyers stove.

Williams Stove. This stove consisted of separate outer and inner casings that were hinged to each other. A detachable cover, provided with two flanges, fitted over the upper edges of the outer casing. The stove was patented by J. S. Williams, of Philadelphia.

Woodbury Stove. Consisting of a fire chamber in two sections and a stovepipe in five pieces, this stove could be disassembled and compactly packed.

SWORD BELTS, ARMY. In the Union army, the regulation sword belt was a waist belt, 1½ to 2 inches wide, that was worn over the sash. The sword was suspended from the belt by slings made of the same material as the belt.

The belt for general officers was made of Russian leather, with three stripes of gold embroidery; the slings were embroidered on both sides, as well. Other officers and noncommissioned officers wore a belt of black leather, unembellished. The belt for enlisted men was similar to that of junior officers.

In addition, a wide variety of sword belts were privately manufactured in the North, following the above basic guidelines.

For all Union officers and enlisted men, the regulation sword-belt plate was gilt, rectangular, and 2 inches wide, with a raised bright rim. A silver wreath of laurel encircled the U.S. coat of arms. Both the motto "E Pluribus Unum" and the stars on the coat of arms were silver.

Confederate army sword belts were identical to the regulation Union belts, with the same distinctions made according to rank. The Confederate sword-belt plate was the same as the Union belt plate, except that it had a silver wreath of laurel encircling the Confederate coat of arms.

SWORD BELTS, NAVY. The sword belt for U.S. navy officers and the sling were made of black glazed leather. The belt plate was yellow gilt in front and measured 2 inches in diameter. The belt was worn over the coat.

SWORDS, ARMY, CONFEDERATE. Swords and other edged weapons were made at a number of locations in the South. All types of U.S. edged weapons were copied. In addition, the Confederacy imported various swords and sabers.

The names of manufacturers most commonly found on Confederate edged weapons include the following: Boyle, Gamble and Mac Fee, Richmond; Campbell and Co., London; College Hill Arsenal, Nashville; James Conning, Mobile; Louis Froelich, Keansville, North Carolina; Wm. Glaze and Co.,

Union cavalry charges at a reenactment of the Battle of Gettysburg. On the third day of the battle, July 3, 1863, cavalry led by General George Armstrong Custer prevented J. E. B. Stuart's rebel cavalry from attacking the Union rear during Pickett's Charge. (CT)

Columbia, South Carolina; Thomas Griswold and Co., New Orleans; Halfman and Taylor, Montgomery; L. Harman and Bro., Columbia, Georgia; Isaac's and Co., London; E. J. Johnston and Co., Macon; Kraft, Goldschmidt and Kraft, Columbia, South Carolina; Leech and Rignon, Memphis; W. J. McElroy, Macon; Mitchell and Tyler Co., Richmond; and Robert Mole and Co., Birmingham, England.

SWORDS, ARMY, FEDERAL. Swords and sabers used in the Civil War were designed for use in combat, not in ceremonies. Still, they retained their peacetime role of designating rank and, in some instances, branch of service.

Swords and sword belts were worn upon all occasions of duty. When not on military duty, officers could wear swords of honor or the prescribed sword, with a scabbard of gilt or of leather with gilt mountings.

SWORDS, NAVY, FEDERAL. In 1852, the U.S. navy adopted a sword that, with only very minor variations, was worn until swords were no longer part of the naval uniform. Regulations specified that "for all officers there shall be a cut-and-thrust blade, not less than 26 nor more than 29 inches long, with a half-basket hilt and a white grip." Scabbards were made of black leather, with mountings of yellow gilt.

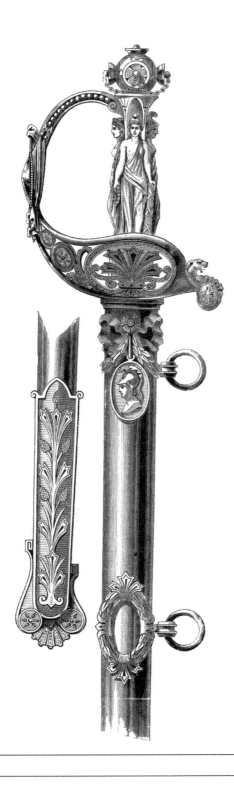

Presentation swords to officers were elaborate almost beyond belief, sometimes encrusted with jewels with solid silver scabbards. Such a sword, presented to Robert E. Lee, is displayed in the Museum of the Confederacy in Richmond. (NA)

T

TELEGRAPH EQUIPMENT. Both Union and Confederate telegraph services became well developed during the war.

The U.S. Military-Telegraph Corps devised a field telegraph system consisting of reels of insulated cable strong enough to resist cannon wheels. These reels, which were carried on the backs of mules, played out the wire over the fields, where it was raised on lances or trees. Compact portable electric batteries were transported in battery wagons constructed for the purpose and were frequently set up under tent flies in close proximity to the commander's headquarters.

Only a few items actually used in the telegraph services exist today, either in museums or in private collections. Both sides used relatively simple coding devices, a few of which survived the war.

The Union army began using the telegraph after First Manassas, and by the end of the war, the U.S. Military-Telegraph Corps was using more than 6,500 miles of wire. Each side tapped the other's lines, and each used code. Union telegraphers broke the Confederate code; Confederate telegraphers never solved the union cipher. (NA)

The interior of a Union officer's tent suggests that his life in the field was not without creature comfort. His tent, however, could be sweltering in the summer and offered neither protection from insects nor running water. The chairs and the bed suggest that the occupant was of field grade, a major or above. (NA)

TENTS. The Federal army used a variety of tents in the field and in semi-permanent camps. Confederate tents were ordinary wall tents, often captured from the Union army or purchased from civilian sources.

"A" Tent. The "A," or wedge, tent was one of the most commonly used by the North. It was a canvas tent stretched over a horizontal bar about 6 feet long, which was supported on two upright posts. When pitched, this tent covered about 50 square feet. The end of the tent bore a resemblance to the letter A—hence its name.

The "A" tent was made to hold four men comfortably, but often it held six, which required that all men in the tent turn over at the same time. "A" tents were used extensively by the Union during the first two years of the war, but like Sibley tents, they required too much wagon transportation to be practical for field use. As a result, they were turned over to training camps, troop depots, and permanently located troops.

Brecht Tent. T. C. Brecht, a Union officer, patented a combination tent, cloak, and bed. It consisted of a sheet of water- and airtight fabric, doubled so it could be inflated and thus form a bed or a mattress. It could be used as a tent or a cloak when not inflated.

Day Shelter Tent. An excellent tent, made of gutta-percha cloth, was designed by Horace Day, of New York. In some respects, it was superior to the Rider tent-knapsack, but neither saw much service.

John's Tent-Knapsack. Patented by a Federal officer named William B. John, this knapsack could be separated from its slings, which could then be hooked together to permit the knapsack to function as a shelter tent or to hold the soldier's kit while on the march.

Poncho Tent. Horace Day invented this tent and sold it in his New York City establishment for $6.50 if treated with enamel paint or for $10 if water-proofed with rubber. Many soldiers preferred the poncho tent to the rubber blanket and found it warmer than the shelter tent. The poncho tent, which weighed 7 pounds, consisted of three rubber blankets that could be converted into a sleeping tent capable of housing three men.

Shelter Tent. Also known as the dog tent or the pup tent, the shelter tent was the one most commonly used by the Union. Soldiers called it a dog tent because, they claimed, when pitched, it would accommodate only a dog, and a small one at that.

The shelter tent was invented late in 1861. Most shelter tents were made of cotton drilling, although some were made of light duck or rubber. During the first year of the war alone, the U.S. army used more than 300,000 of these tents.

Infantry soldiers pitched their shelter tents by sticking two muskets with bayonets fixed erect into the ground. A guy rope was then stretched between the trigger guards of the muskets, serving as a ridge pole.

Artillerymen pitched their shelter tents over a horizontal bar supported by two uprights. The framework was made from thin fence rails or saplings cut for the purpose. When the men went into winter quarters, their shelter tents were used as roofs until other material could be obtained.

Sibley, or Bell, Tent. The inventor of this tent, Herbert Sibley, accompanied Union General John Fremont on an exploration out West, where he noted the advantages of the Indian teepee—a wigwam made of poles covered with skins and with fire in the center. Sibley, a West Pointer, eventually left the Union army to join the Confederate army, where he rose to the rank of

The most common tent used by the Union army was the shelter tent, which soldiers called a pup tent or dog tent, apparently because it could accommodate only a small dog comfortably. The shelter tent offered little shelter from the elements, and none from insects. (NA)

The Sibley tent, patterned after an Indian wigwam, was made of poles covered with canvas with an opening at the top to carry off the smoke of a cooking fire. The tent could accommodate 12 men comfortably. It was also called a bell tent. (NA)

brigadier general, but he is remembered for inventing the tent that bore his name.

Because of its resemblance to a huge bell, the Sibley was sometimes called a bell tent. It measured 18 feet in diameter and 12 feet high and was supported by a single pole that rested on an iron tripod, by means of which the tent could be tightened or slackened. At the top was a circular opening, about a foot in diameter, that allowed for ventilation and for passing a stovepipe through in cool weather. The stovepipe connected with the famous Sibley stove. A small piece of canvas, called a cap, to which was attached two long guys, covered the opening in stormy weather. The Sibley tent could house 12 men comfortably, but it was much too cumbersome for active field operations. During the war, the U.S. army used 43,935 Sibley tents.

Wall, or Hospital, Tent. This unusual tent had four upright sides, or walls, and because of the increased headroom, it was much more comfortable than tents of other types. Men could stand erect and move about with considerable freedom in the wall tent, which made it particularly suitable for field hospital use.

Wall tents were made in different sizes. The ones used as field hospitals were large, accommodating from 6 to 20 patients. Often, two of these were joined to form a long double-tent that had a central corridor running its entire length between a double row of cots.

Smaller wall tents were commonly used by commissioned officers. While the Army of the Potomac was on the Peninsula, General George B. McClellan issued an order prescribing wall tents for general, field, and staff officers. Each line officer was allowed a single shelter tent.

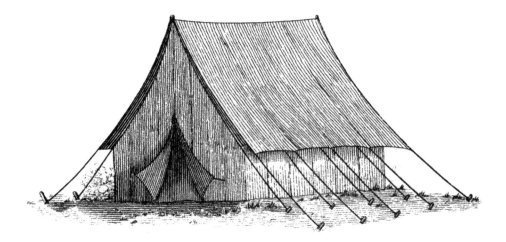

The wall tent was used by Union officers in the field. Larger versions were used as hospital tents and could shelter up to 20 patients lying on two rows of cots. By lifting the flaps, wall tents could be linked to enclose larger areas. (NA)

U

UNIFORMS, ARMY, CONFEDERATE. Although there were regulation Confederate army uniforms, only a few fortunate soldiers wore them in 1861 and 1862, and fewer still as the war continued. The government was never able to furnish sufficient uniforms, and the problem was solved only partially at the state level. Many early volunteers wore militia clothing, and sometimes a local company would wear uniforms purchased by the company commander. Many volunteers were told to furnish their own clothing.

Colors ranged from the gaudy hues of the Louisiana Zouaves' uniforms to the yellowish brown (called butternut) of uniforms dyed with a solution of copperas and walnut hulls. Trousers were usually gray, but shirts were of all colors and materials. Most soldiers wore hats, although caps were prescribed by the regulations.

Some soldiers wore captured Federal uniforms, although the practice was discouraged. "Yankee overcoats" were particularly popular. In some commands, the men dyed their captured clothing.

States tended to keep uniforms for the use of units from that state. While Lee's men were freezing in the trenches at Petersburg, the governor of North Carolina refused to release 92,000 uniforms, blankets, and other necessities to the general cause, although North Carolina troops were all well uniformed.

The Confederate regulation uniform of 1861 was as follows.

Enlisted Man's Uniform.

Coat. The uniform coat for the enlisted man was a tunic made of cadet gray cloth, with the skirt extending halfway between the hip and the knee. The tunic had two rows of buttons on the breast; a stand-up collar; cuffs that buttoned; and pockets in the folds of the skirts. As with the officer's coat, the edges, collar, and cuffs of the tunic varied in color to indicate branch of service.

Headgear. Troops wore a forage cap similar to the officer's cap, with a band

Most Confederate regiments equipped themselves locally, and when uniforms and equipment wore out, it was often up to the private soldier to replace them. Uniforms were in many colors from gray to brown to butternut. Shown is a first sergeant's frock coat and kepi. (MOC)

of dark blue and the arms of service distinguished by the color of the sides and crown: red for artillery, yellow for cavalry, and light blue for infantry. The number of the regiment, in yellow metal, was worn in front.

In hot weather, a white duck or linen cover, known as a havelock, was worn on the cap, with the apron falling behind to protect the ears and neck from the sun. In winter or in bad weather, an oil skin cover was worn, with the apron falling over the coat collar.

Trousers. The uniform trousers for enlisted men were loose, spreading well over the foot, and were made of light blue cloth.

All sergeants had a stripe of cotton webbing or braid on the outer seam, colored according to arm of service. Other enlisted men had no decoration on the trousers.

Officer's Uniform.

Coat. Officers wore a tunic-style double-breasted coat made of cadet gray cloth that had a skirt that extended halfway between the hip and the knee. The coat had two rows of buttons on the breast; a stand-up collar; buttoned cuffs; and pockets in the folds of the skirt.

The edges, collar, and cuffs of the tunic varied in color, as follows: red for artillery, yellow for cavalry, light blue for infantry, and black for medical.

Headgear. General officers and officers of the general staff and Corps of Engineers wore a chapeau, or cocked hat, of French pattern, usually only on dress occasions.

All officers wore a forage cap similar in form to that of the French kepi. Marks on the cap distinguished rank. The braid extended from the band at the front, back, and both sides to the top of the cap; the center of the crown was embroidered with the same number of braids.

Trousers. Uniform trousers for officers were loose and spread well over the foot. They were light blue for regimental officers and dark blue for all other officers, and they were reinforced for the cavalry.

Officers in the Adjutant General's, the Quartermaster General's, and the Commissary General's Departments and in the Corps of Engineers had one stripe of gold lace. Medical officers had a black velvet stripe with a gold cord on each edge of the stripe. Regimental officers had a stripe of cloth on the

Union army uniforms and headgear included, left to right, a frock coat and trousers of a drum major; a shako of a soldier of a National Guard regiment, and a frock coat of a lieutenant colonel of a volunteer infantry regiment. (USMA)

outer seams, the color according to corps: red for artillery, yellow for cavalry, and dark blue for infantry.

UNIFORMS, ARMY, FEDERAL. Although some states had their own uniform regulations for their troops, the great majority of Federal troops wore uniforms prescribed as follows in *Army Regulations 1861*.

Boots. Boots tended to be confined to mounted personnel, including mounted officers of infantry regiments. Foot soldiers were issued ankle boots, or bootees. Called mudscows or gunboats by the troops, some were so poorly made that they wore out after a month of hard use.

Enlisted Man's Uniform.

Coat. All foot soldiers wore a single-breasted frock coat of dark blue cloth, without plaits, with a skirt and a stand-up collar. The skirt was narrow-lined in the same color and material as the coat. The coat had one row of nine buttons on the breast. The cuffs were pointed and each buttoned. The collar and cuffs were edged with cording—scarlet for artillery, yellow for engineers, sky blue for infantry, and crimson for ordnance and hospital stewards. All enlisted men of the cavalry and light artillery wore a jacket of dark blue cloth.

Fatigue Coat. This was a loose-fitting sack coat made of dark blue flannel. It had a falling collar and was lined with wool in the body.

Headgear. Enlisted men wore a hat made of black felt similar to the officer's hat. The cord was worsted and its color varied according to the branch of the army. It ran two times through a slide and terminated with two tassels. The hat had only one black ostrich feather. A brass insignia of branch was on the front of the hat, with the regiment number and company letter. Like officers, enlisted men wore forage caps of various types.

Overcoat. Mounted troops wore a double-breasted overcoat made of sky blue cloth, with a stand-and-fall collar and a cape. Other enlisted men wore a similar overcoat, except it had a cape to the elbows and was single-breasted.

Sash. A red wool sash was worn over the coat by senior non-commissioned officers.

Trousers. Made of sky blue cloth, sergeants' had a wide stripe; corporals', a narrower stripe. Stripes colors oshowed branch of service.

George B. McClellan, one of many unsuccessful commanders of the Army of the Potomac, poses in the uniform of a Union lieutenant general. Most of the senior officers, North and South, were graduates of West Point and shared a common military tradition. The insignia and design of Union and Confederate uniforms are remarkably similar. (NA)

Militia Uniforms. During the early months of the war, a nearly limitless variety of militia uniforms were worn by both sides. The most photographed Federal militia unit, the 7th Regiment, New York State Militia, wore a gray uniform and a low kepi. Other Northern commands also wore gray uniforms early in the war.

Officer's Uniform.

Coat. Officers were to wear a dark blue frock coat with a stand-up collar and a skirt. Major generals had two rows of buttons on the breast, nine in each row, placed by threes. There were pockets in the folds of the skirt, with one button at the hip and one at the end of the pocket, with the hip button in line with the lowest buttons on the breast. The collar and cuffs were made of dark blue velvet, and the lining was black.

The brigadier general's coat was the same as the major general's, except that it had eight buttons in each row on the breast, placed in pairs. The coat for colonels, lieutenant colonels, and majors had seven buttons in each row on the breast, placed at equal distances. The coat for captains, first and second lieutenants, and medical cadets was like the colonel's, except that it had only one row of nine buttons on the breast, placed at equal distances.

While on undress duty, officers of the light artillery could wear a round jacket made of dark blue cloth and trimmed with scarlet. It had Russian shoulder knots, with the prescribed insignia of rank worked in silver in the center of each knot.

In the field, both officers and the enlisted men who rode horses wore simple, functional spurs. On formal occasions and dress reviews, high-ranking members usually wore gold-plated spurs of fanciful design. The dress spurs shown incorporate an American eagle. (NA)

Headgear. Union army officers wore a hat made of best black felt silk. It was trimmed in gold-and-black cord with acorn-shaped ends. On the right side, the brim looped up and fastened with an eagle, and on the left side were three black ostrich feathers. In front was a gold embroidered wreath on a black felt ground, encircling the letters "U.S."

Officers also wore various forage caps. The McClellan forage cap was a fairly faithful copy of the kepi, but the bummers cap was described as "shapeless as a feed bag." Its leather visor curled up when dry and sagged when wet.

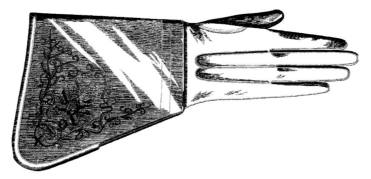

Gauntlets, as gloves of this style are called, were part of the dress uniform of Union army officers. Some, like the one shown here, incorporated elaborate designs. Few Civil War gauntlets survive today. (NA)

Overcoat. Officers wore a cloak coat of dark blue cloth that closed down the breast with four frog buttons of black silk and loops of black silk cord and at the throat with a black silk frog button and a long loop. To indicate rank, each sleeve had a knot of flat black-silk braid

Sash. A silk sash of a color corresponding to rank and branch of service was worn by officers over the coat on all occasions of duty, except stable and fatigue.

Trousers. Federal officers' trousers were made of dark blue cloth. Trousers for officers of the general staff and staff corps had a gold cord along the outer seam, other officers had welts along the seam.

Special Unit Uniforms. Some special units in the Union army wore their own distinctive uniforms.

Berdan's Sharpshooters. The uniform for this unit was a dark green coat, light blue trousers (later exchanged for green trousers), a dark green cap with a black plume, and leather leggings. Buttons were made of hard rubber rather than yellow metal so as not to attract enemy fire. Berdan's Sharpshooters were known as the Green Coats.

Bucktails. The Bucktails (the 13th Pennsylvania Reserves and the 1st Pennsylvania Rifles) wore bucktails (made from the tails of deer) in their forage caps.

Garibaldi Guards. This Italian-American unit, officially called the 39th New York Infantry, wore a very dark greenish blue uniform and a flat-brimmed, round-top hat decorated with cock's feathers, which were copied from the Italian army uniform.

Zouaves. Most Zouave units were from the East, primarily New York, though a few units were raised in the Midwest and the South. All wore modified Zouave uniforms. Federal army Zouave officers wore a regulation-style frock coat with red trousers and distinctive headgear of the same general color and cut as that worn by their enlisted men.

Ellsworth's Chicago Zouaves wore a bright red chasseur cap with gold braid, a light blue shirt with moiré antique facings, a dark blue jacket with orange and red trimmings and brass bell buttons, a red sash, loose red trousers, russet leather leggings, and a white waist belt. The uniform was comfortable as well as colorful.

Officially called Baxter's 72nd Pennsylvania Infantry, the Philadelphia Fire Zouaves were raised in 1861. Of the original 1,600 men in the unit, 988 were killed, wounded, or missing in action. Their uniform was a modified Zouave, consisting primarily of Zouave trousers and leggings but retaining the regulation cap rather than using the fez. Of special interest to collectors is the regiment's unique cartridge-box plate, marked with the block letters "PFZ."

Birney's Zouaves, or the 23rd Pennsylvania Infantry, went to war in a dark blue Zouave uniform. After six months in the field, the uniforms were worn out and were replaced with the regulation Union army uniform.

A guide dressed in a period sailor's uniform, a fife in his belt, takes part in a living history program at the Richmond National Battlefield. Navy gunboats would steam up the navigable rivers and employ their firepower in support of the ground troops. (CT)

The 9th New York Infantry, known as Hawkin's Zouaves, wore a uniform of army blue, with trousers slightly full and plaited at the waist, a magenta braid down the sash, white leggings, and a red fez with a blue tassel. One observer noted: "It was totally different from the uniforms issued by the United States authorities, and no nattier one was worn by any body of troops in the service.

Collis's Zouaves was the 114th Pennsylvania Infantry. Though many Zouave regiments were required to wear the regulation army uniform as soon as their Zouave uniforms wore out, Collis's troops were permitted to wear their unique uniforms throughout the war. The 114th's uniform consisted of red pants, Zouave jacket, white leggings, blue sash, and white turban.

UNIFORMS, NAVY, CONFEDERATE.

Enlisted Man's Uniform. In the Confederate navy, the uniform was a gray jacket with white duck collar and cuffs, gray trousers, a black hat, a black silk neckerchief, and black shoes. In warm weather, an enlisted man wore a white frock with blue cotton collar and cuffs, white trousers, a black or white hat, a black silk neckerchief, and black shoes. A thick gray cap without a visor was worn at sea.

Senior petty officers wore a foul anchor embroidered in black silk on the right sleeve of the gray jacket and the same device embroidered in blue silk on the right sleeve of the white frock. Other petty officers wore the same device on the left sleeve.

Officer's Uniform.

Cap. For all officers, the cap was made of steel gray cloth with a patent-leather visor. A flag officer's cap had a foul anchor in a wreath of oak leaves, with four gold stars on the front of the cap above a 1¾-inch band of gold. A captain wore the same, except that there were three stars; a commander wore two stars; a lieutenant, one; a master, no star; and a midshipman, a foul anchor without the wreath.

Coat. A flag officer wore a gray frock coat lined with black silk. The coat had two rows of nine buttons and a rolling collar. A stripe of gold lace was below the cuff seam, and three stripes of gold lace were above the cuff.

A captain wore the same, except that there were three stripes of lace around the sleeve and cuff. A commander had two stripes around the sleeve. A lieutenant had one stripe of gold lace. A midshipman's coat had no lace.

Overcoat. All officers wore a gray double-breasted overcoat, with a rolling collar. Gray cloaks were worn in boats.

Trousers. All officers wore trousers made of steel gray cloth or white drill.

UNIFORMS, NAVY, FEDERAL.

Enlisted Man's Uniform. The uniform for petty officers and seamen was a blue woolen frock or jacket, blue trousers, a black hat, a black silk neckerchief, and black shoes or boots. In warm weather, the uniform consisted of a white frock coat with blue cotton collar and cuffs, white trousers, a black or white hat, a black neckerchief, and black shoes.

Officer's Uniform. An officer's full dress uniform consisted of frock coat, epaulettes, plain pantaloons, cocked hat, and sword. During the war, the epaulettes and cocked hat were dispensed with. Undress was the same as full dress but without the epaulettes and cocked hat and with or without the sword.

Cap. The cap was made of dark blue cloth and had a black patent-leather visor. A black cover was worn over the top in rainy weather. The cap ornament had a gold wreath of oak and olive branches, which enclosed the following devices: rear admiral—two silver stars; commodore down through ensign—a silver foul anchor.

Coat. The navy blue frock coat was double-breasted with two rows of nine buttons. The skirt was full, with one button behind on each hip and one near the bottom of each fold.

Jacket. All officers wore jackets as "service" dress. They were navy blue, single- or double-breasted, with a rolling collar. They had the same number of, buttons on the breast, similar lace on the cuffs, and the same shoulder straps as did the coat.

Overcoat. The overcoat and cape was of dark blue beaver with a skirt. The cape was shorter and could be removed to form a separate garment. On the collars were the following devices: rear-admiral—two silver stars;

David Farragut, who joined the navy at the age of 10, and was commander of the fleets at New Orleans, Vicksburg, and Mobile, where his command "Damn the torpedoes! Full speed ahead!" thrilled the nation, cuts a dashing figure in the uniform of a full admiral in the Union navy, a rank that was created especially to honor him. (NA)

commodore—one silver star; captain—a silver eagle; commander—a silver leaf; lieutenant-commander—a gold leaf; lieutenant—two silver bars; master—one silver bar; and ensign—a small gold cord on the front edge of the collar.

Pantaloons. All officers wore pantaloons, either navy blue or white. In the tropics, white pantaloons were worn in all seasons.

Union naval officers wore the navy officer's cap, upper left, while at sea and performing routine chores ashore. The navy chapeau, lower right, was reserved for inspections and other formal occasions. (NA)

W

WRITING EQUIPMENT. Most Union soldiers wrote letters home or had friends write their letters for them. At first, they used stamps on their letters, but later in the war, postage was waived for soldiers if they wrote on the envelope "Soldier's Letter." A bit of doggerel on one envelope said:

> Soldier's letter, nary read,
>
> Hardtack and no soft bread,
>
> Postmaster please put it through,
>
> I've nary a cent, but six months due.

Patriotic envelopes that were used in the war are popular with collectors today. While the main motif was always patriotic, the variations on this theme

To help pay for the war, a sales tax was instituted in the summer of 1864. Merchants purchased revenue stamps at the post office and affixed them to the items they sold. Shown above are stamps affixed to the back of studio photographs, usually canceled with the photographer's initials. (GG)

were seemingly endless. Many had the American eagle with the motto "The Union. It must and shall be preserved!" Others had portraits of past heroes like George Washington or contemporary figures like President Lincoln or General McClellan. Caricatures of Jefferson Davis and other Confederate leaders were common, as well. Much rarer were envelopes with brightly colored maps. The rarest of all were envelopes made for specific units, such as the 1st Ohio Battery or the 24th Massachusetts Volunteers.

Letter-writing equipment was sold by sutlers at the front. Stationery ranged from plane coarse yellow paper to excellent writing paper decorated with the same cartoons and slogans as the envelopes. The U.S. Christian Commission, an offshoot of the YMCA, furnished paper and envelopes to soldiers free of charge. Commission envelopes bore the stamp or the name of the commission and "Soldier's Letter" in one corner.

Soldiers had to buy their own ink, mainly from sutlers, although ink was issued to units for official correspondence. Government ink was issued in glass bottles with glass stoppers.

This novelty photograph of a camp photographer holding his camera could have been taken today at a Civil War reenactment. Often, Polaroid photographs of authentic-looking reenactors are sepia-toned, placed in old frames, and sold to naive collectors as authentic antiques. (GG)

Appendix A
GETTING STARTED

HOW TO BE A SAVVY COLLECTOR

Beginning collectors should beware. It's easy to pay too much for an authentic artifact, and fakes are still being sold to the unsuspecting. Getting stung is a blow to the ego as well as to your pocketbook. But by following a few simple rules, even a rank novice can stay out of trouble.

Before you start to collect Civil War artifacts, collect some reference books on the subject. The more you know, the more savvy you will be at collecting.

Take every opportunity to talk with established collectors, dealers, and curators. Most are glad to help neophytes. Question them, and pay close attention to their answers. Don't try to impress them with your knowledge—get them to share their knowledge with you.

Get a feel for what's out there and what it costs. Go to auctions. Go to expositions. Read the periodicals for collectors. Occasionally, a periodical will print a warning about fakes on the market. Clip warnings for future reference.

Do your homework before you go shopping for a particular item. If, for instance, you want to buy a revolver, find a museum or a collector and look at the revolvers in that collection. Learn what to look for and what to ask about revolvers. Know, for example, that a Colt Third Model Dragoon percussion revolver in good condition can cost $10,000 or more, while a Starr revolver can cost about $1,000.

Buy only from auction houses, collectors, and dealers you know to be reputable and that will stand behind anything they sell to you. Don't be afraid to ask questions before you buy. Ask the seller if he will give you a written guarantee of authenticity. Most reputable dealers will.

If you think you've found a bargain or a rare piece at a questionable source, ask an established collector to check it out before you buy. Be especially wary if the price is quite low. A price that is out of line usually is an indication that the piece is not authentic. And *always* get a second opinion from an expert you trust before spending a lot of money.

Diaries of soldiers are among the prized possessions of Civil War collector of E. D. Simes. Most collectors specialize—firearms, uniforms, buttons, medals, recruiting posters, medical equipment, daguerreotypes, or musical instruments—whatever strikes their fancy. (CT)

Beware of reproductions. Sometimes they can fool all but the most knowledgeable.

Civil War newspapers with stories about big battles or momentous events have been reproduced many times. For example, the front page of the *New York Herald* that carried the news of President Lincoln's assassination was reproduced as a promotional stunt for the 1892 Colombian Exposition. Now, those reproductions are sufficiently aged and yellowed to pass for originals. Also beware of the July 4, 1863, *Vicksburg Daily Citizen* printed on wallpaper, and the August 9, 1862, *Chattanooga Rebel*. Both were reprinted in the early 1890s and often fool experts. A rule of thumb: Legitimate editions of Union newspapers can still be found in the $10 range, while the far rarer C.S.A. newspapers fetch $100 and up.

Both Currier and Ives and Kurz and Allison prints have been reproduced. The best way to detect a reproduction is to view the print under a magnifying glass and look for a pattern, known as moiré, of multicolored geometric rings and dots.

Cast-iron mechanical banks have been reproduced, most notably the "Artillery Bank," both the Union and Confederate versions. If a bank has a bust of Lincoln, General Robert E. Lee, or General Ulysses S. Grant, it was manufactured in the late 1800s. No such banks date from the Civil War. Castiron match safes with figures of Grant and U.S. politician Horace Greeley have been reproduced in recent years. The reproductions have the bust image wired to the back plate; the originals were riveted.

Civil War badges have been copied, and many originals have been doctored. Look for mismatched metal, new solder, replaced pins, or other signs of cosmetic tampering.

Any celluloid or lithographed button picturing a president before William McKinley is a commemorative item produced at a later date.

Many Civil War paper photographs are copies—photographs of photographs—but they are easy to spot because they lack clarity and contrast. A copy is worth about a third as much as the original.

Finally, many artifacts have been repainted or retouched, often by wellmeaning collectors who believe this enhances them aesthetically. Whether it does is debatable, but it is a fact that the value of a repaint is about half that of an all-original.

A photographer of the Civil War era had to be a do-it-yourself part chemist and part furniture mover. Small cameras and labs that processed films for the amateur were decades away. (GG)

CARING FOR YOUR ARTIFACTS

Ephemera, a museum term for printed or handwritten paper memorabilia, can be damaged by high temperature and high humidity. However, summer air conditioning and winter heating usually are sufficient to keep them from being damaged. Avoid handling papers, or any delicate artifacts, because bare hands carry oil and dirt that can cause deterioration. If you must handle papers, wear cotton gloves, and always hold them with two hands. Don't fold important papers, either. It weakens the fibers and leads to rips or tears across the creases. Never use paper clips, staples, or rubber bands, and avoid adhesive tape. Put paper items in Mylar sleeves for display. Back them with acid-free mats only, and in framing, avoid direct contact with the glass. Use a vinyl eraser, rubbing lightly and in only one direction.

Textiles from the Civil War period are fragile and as susceptible to damage as paper. Wear clean cotton gloves when handling delicate materials. Don't store textiles in plastic bags or in places where extreme temperatures exist. A flat textile is best stored rolled in an acid-free tube. If a textile must be folded, place acid-free tissue between the folds. A small hand–held vacuum may be used to clean dust and other matter from small textiles. To vacuum, place a screen over the fabric and cover the vacuum nozzle with cheesecloth before passing it over the fabric.

Leather should be preserved and kept free from cracking by periodically applying an approved compound. (Though most conservators agree on this, some advise against applying anything.) Two acceptable leather dressings are Picards and British Museum. Apply the dressing to the surface, wipe away the excess, let the rest dry overnight, and then buff lightly. When working with leather book bindings, insert cardboard barriers to prevent the oil from coming in contact with the paper pages.

Glassware and *ceramics* should be handled carefully and cleaned in a plastic dishpan with warm, soapy water and a little vinegar. Avoid washing glassware with enamel paint on its surface. Trying to repair cracks or breakage yourself invites disaster. If the item is valuable, have it repaired by a professional conservator.

Metalware—saber or firearm, cast-iron or tinplate—also should be handled with gloves. Fingerprints on metal lead quickly to rust. Clean cast- or wrought-iron items with 0000-grade steel wool and a light-grade mineral oil. Clean copper and brass with Golden Glow, manufactured by Ball and Ball; experts say Brasso has too much ammonia for artifacts. Clean pewter with Noxon and silver with Tarni-Shield, and store both in treated bags available from jewelry stores. Never store silver in plastic bags. Rinse any polished metal, except iron, in warm water and Ivory soap to soften the residue of old polish, then rinse in denatured alcohol and pat dry before applying new polish.

KP duty was an unpleasant part of army life then as now. At a Maryland reenactment, members of Battery B, 2nd Illinois Light Artillery, wash the dishes. Some antiques, such as the tinware shown here, are best left on display, safely at home. No doubt these enthusiasts are using high-quality reproductions. (CT)

Appendix B
WHERE TO BUY

AUCTION HOUSES

Bill Bertoia Auctions, 2413 Madison Ave., Vineland, NJ 08360, 609-692-1881. Banks, games, and toys.

Butterfield & Butterfield, 220 San Bruno Ave., San Francisco, CA 94103, 415-861-7500; or 7601 Sunset Blvd., Los Angeles, CA 90046, 213-850-7500. Occasional Civil War auctions.

Christie's East, 219 E. 67th St., New York, NY 10021, 212-570-4141. Americana, toys, and vintage advertising.

Conestoga Auction Co., Inc., P.O. Box 1, Manheim, PA 17545, 717-898-7284.

J. C. Divine Gallery, Milford, NH 03055, 603-673-4967. Civil War regalia and weaponry.

William "Pete" Harvey Auctions, 1270 Rte. 28 A, P.O. Box 280, Calumet, MA 02534, 509-540-0660. Accessories, uniforms, and weaponry.

James D. Julia, Inc., P.O. Box 830, Fairfield, ME 04937, 207-453-7125. Americana, firearms, toys, and vintage advertising.

Rick Opfer Auctioneering, Inc., 1919 Greenspring Dr., Timonium, MD 21093, 301-252-5035. Americana, black memorabilia, toys, and vintage advertising.

Swann Galleries, Inc., 104 E. 24th St., New York, NY 10010, 212-254-4710. Frequent auctions with Civil War ephemera, photography, and posters.

A Union general might have this gold embroidered American eagle sewn on his saddle blanket. (NA)

CATALOG HOUSES

Al Anderson, P.O. Box 644, Troy, OH 45373, 513-339-0850. Political memorabilia, especially badges and pinbacks.

Tom French, 1840 41st Ave., #102-128, Capitola, CA 95010, 408-426-9096. Patriotic and political material.

David Frent, P.O. Box 455, Oakhurst, NJ 07755, 908-922-0786. Political memorabilia, especially badges, pinbacks, and ribbons.

Harmer Rooke Galleries, 32 E. 57th St., New York, NY 10022, 212-751-1900. Absentee auctions. Civil War and President Lincoln memorabilia, medical antiques, photographs, and vintage advertising.

Historicana, Robert W. Coup, 1632 Roberts Rd., Lancaster, PA 18601, 717-291-1037. Patriotic and political material.

Jefferson Rarities Collection, 2400 Jefferson Hwy., Jefferson, LA 70121, 800-877-8847. Autographs, books, and manuscripts.

Manion's International Auction House, Inc., Box 12214, Kansas City, KS 66112, 913-299-6692. Documents, ephemera, medals, uniforms, and weaponry.

Political Gallery, 1236 88th St., Indianapolis, IN 46260, 317-257-0863. Some Civil War advertising and political memorabilia.

DEALERS IN ANTIQUES

This list includes a generous sampling of the established dealers that specialize in Civil War relics and memorabilia. All but a few sell by mail order. Write or call for their catalogs or lists.

American Military Antiques, 8398 Court Ave., Ellicott City, MD 21073, 410-465-6827.

Mike Brackin, P.O. Box 23, Manchester, CT 06040.

The Carolina Gallery, 113 Church St., Waynesville, NC 28786, 704-586-4960.

Catlett Brothers, Rte. 1, P.O. Box 170, Fredericksburg, VA 22401, 703-786-7600.

Cedar Creek Relic Shop, P.O. Box 232, Middletown, VA 22645, 703-869-5207.

Lawrence Christopher, 4773 Tammey Dr. NE, Dalton, GA 30720, 706-226-8894.

Civil War Antiques, P.O. Box 87, Sylvania, OH 43560.

Confederate Brass, Rte. 2, Box 139, Fairfax, SC 28827, 803-632-3083.

Confederate Memorabilia, P.O. Box 397, Fairfax, VA 22030, 703-631-9518.

Confederate States Metal Detectors, 29025 Government St., Baton Rouge, LA 70806.

Henry Deeks, P.O. Box 1500, East Arlington, MA, 02174.

George C. Esker III Antiques, P.O. Box 100, LaPlace, LA 70069, 504-887-5802.

Falmouth Trading Post, 536 Cambridge St., Fredericksburg, VA 22401, 703-371-3309.

The Galvanized Yankee, 1016 Lafayette Blvd., Fredericksburg, VA 22401, 703-373-1886.

Peter C. George, P.O. Box 74, Mechanicsville, VA 23111, 804-321-7272.

Will Gorges, 308 Simmons St., New Bern, NC 28562, 919-636-3039.

Dennis Gregg, P.O. Box 432, Braddock Heights, MD 21714, 301-293-6141.

Gunsight Antiques, P.O. Box 1056, Westbtrook, ME 04092, 207-839-3825.

A soldier of Company D, Rhode Island 2nd Infantry, poses beside his tent. Revolvers were issued only to officers, and the one in his belt was either brought from home or found on the battlefield. It would be a much more effective weapon at close quarters than the muzzle-loading musket he is holding. (NA)

Larry and Debbie Hicklen, Rte. 10, Old Nashville Hwy., Murfreesboro, TN 37130, 615-893-3470.

The Horse Soldier Shop, 777 Baltimore Ave., Gettysburg, PA 17310, 717-334-0347.

Johnny Reb's Outpost, 2980 Austin Peay Hwy., Memphis, TN 38128, 901-372-7385.

J. Reb's "Chickamauga Battlefield" Civil War Relic Gallery, 759 Battlefield Pkwy., Suite 14, Fort Oglethorpe, GA 30742, 706-866-2005.

Kennesaw Mountain Military Antiques, 1810 Old Hwy. 41, Kennesaw, GA 30144, 404-424-JACK.

Michael D. Kramer, 269 Mt. Kemble Ave., Morristown, NJ 07960, 212-807-7550.

L & G Early Arms, P.O. Box 113, Amelia, OH 45102.

Jeffrey Lea, 6922 Pam Dr., Millington, TN 38053, 901-873-3064.

Lewis Leigh, Jr., P.O. Box 397, Fairfax, VA 22030, 703-631-9518.

Dennis E. Lowe, RD #2, Box 2699A, Hamburg, PA 19526.

Maryland Line Trader, P.O. Box 190, Lithicum Heights, MD 21090.

Paul Millikan, The Manual of Arms, P.O. Box 372, Mattawan, MI 49071.

Steve E. Mullinax, 433 McCurdy Rd., Villa Rica, GA 30180.

R. E. Neville, 3863 Old Shell Rd., Mobile, AL 36608, 205-478-6434.

Alex Peck, P.O. Box 710, Charleston, IL 61920, 217-348-1009.

The Picket Post, 401 William St., Fredericksburg, VA 22401, 703-371-7703.

Plainsman Gun Shop, 22168 Hillview Dr., Barrington, IL 60010.

The Powder Horn Gun Shop, Inc., 200 W. Washington St., P.O. Box 1001, Middleburg, VA 22117, 703-687-6628.

The Regimental Quartermaster, P.O. Box 553, Hatboro, PA 19040.

Richmond Arsenal, 7605 Midlothian Tnpk., Richmond, VA 23235, 804-272-4570.

Stone Mountain Relics, Inc., 968 Main St., Stone Mountain, GA 30083, 404-469-1425.

Stone's River Bullets, 1302 Dow St., Murfreesboro, TN 37130, 615-896-4860.

Sutler's Wagon, P.O. Box 5, Cambridge, MA 02139.

Sword & Saber, P.O. Box 4417, Gettysburg, PA 17325.

Yesterday, 3511 Old Nashville Hwy., Murfreesboro, TN 37129, 615-893-3470.

The following antique dealers keep mailing lists and will periodically send you information on items they have for sale. Write or call to have your name added to their mailing lists.

William Bopp, Washington Sq., P.O. Box 33, Walpole, NH 03608. Early tin and paper toys.

Civil War Images, P.O. Box 2260, Acton, MA 01720, 508-263-1861. Photographs.

Doug Jordan, Box 20194, St. Petersburg, FL 33742. Civil War and other early photographs.

Profiles in History, Joseph M. Maddalena, 345 N. Maple Dr., Suite 202, Beverly Hills, CA 90210, 800-942-8856. Autographs.

University Archives, 600 Summer St., Stamford, CT 06901, 800-237-5692.

U.S. Gatling Gun. The Gatling gun was the first true machine gun used successfully in wartime. It was a hand-crank-operated weapon with six barrels revolving around a central shaft, capable of firing 600 rounds a minute. Early models were expensive and had many drawbacks. (USMA)

DEALERS IN BOOKS

ABCDEF Books, 726 N. Hanover St., Carlisle PA 17013.

Abraham Lincoln Book Shop, 18 E. Chestnut St., Chicago, IL 60610.

Articles of War, 8806 Bronx Ave., Skokie, IL 60077.

Bacon Race Books, 3717 Pleasant Ridge Rd., Annandale, VA 22003.

Bohemian Brigade Book Shop, 8705 Vultee Lane, Knoxville, TN 37923.

Broadfoot Publishing Co., P.O. Box 508, Rte. 4, Wilmington, NC 28405.

Butternut and Blue, 3411 Northwind Rd., Baltimore, MD 21234, 301-256-9220.

Camp Pope Bookshop, P.O. Box 2232, Iowa City, IA 52254.

The Carolina Trader, P.O. Box 769, Monroe, NC 28110.

The Conflict, P.O. Box 689, 213 Steinwehr Ave., Gettysburg, PA 17325.

Farnsworth House Military Impressions, 401 Baltimore St., Gettysburg, PA 17325, 717-334-8838.

The Galvanized Yankee Bookshop, P.O. Box 37, South Conway, NH 03813.

The Guild Bindery Press, P.O. Box 2071, Lakeway Station, Paris, TN 38242.

Heritage Books, Inc., 1540 E. Pointer Ridge Pl., Bowie, MD 20715, 301-390-7708.

Heritage Trails, P.O. Box 307, Turbotville, PA 17772.

Longstreet House, P.O. Box 730, Heightstown, NY 08520.

McGowan Book Company, P.O. Box 222, Chapel Hill, NC 27514.

The Military Bookman, 29 E. 93rd St., New York, NY 10128, 212-348-1280.

Morningside Bookshop, P.O. Box 1087, 260 Oak St., Dayton, OH 45401.

The Mt. Sterling Rebel, P.O. Box 481, Mt. Sterling, KY 40353.

"Old Army" Books, P.O. Box 24652, Lexington, KY 40524.

Old Favorites Bookshop, 610 N. Sheppard St., Richmond, VA 23221, 804-355-2437.

Old Soldier Books, Inc., 18779B N. Frederick Ave., Gaithersburg, MD 20879, 301-963-2929.

Owen's Civil War Books, 2728 Tinsley, Richmond, VA 23235, 804-272-8888.

Frank E. Reynolds Old Books, P.O. Box 805, Newburyport, MA 01950.
Stone Mountain Relics, Inc., 968 Main St., Stone Mountain, GA 30083, 770-469-1425.
Wolf's Head Books, P.O. Box 1020, Morgantown, WV 26507.

DEALERS IN COLLECTIBLES

A number of contemporary artists now specialize in the Civil War, creating prints depicting battle and camp scenes and portraits of popular leaders. Among the best artists working in this field are Lisa S. Brown, John Duillo, Peter W. Gaut, Michael Gnatek, Jr., Ken Hendricksen, Tom Lovell, Keith A. Rocco, Don Stivers, John Paul Strain, and Don Troiani. Their prints are produced in limited editions and qualify as works of art, which means they could increase in value over time. Unframed prints range in price from $75 to $200 each; framed prints, from $150 to $300 each. A few prints of an edition are released as artist's proofs and usually command an additional $25 to $50 each.

Small sculptures of leaders and battle scenes are sold by mail and in a number of art galleries. Among the artists who specialize in Civil War sculptures are Karl Anderson, Francis Barnum, Gary Casteel, Jennifer Grisham, Thomas Krebs, James Muir, and Ron Tunison. Most such sculpures are in the $100 to $300 range.

Plates are also popular collectibles. A recent example was a limited-edition plate honoring General Robert E. Lee designed by artist John Paul Strain and produced by the Bradford Exchange. Another, by Mort Kunstler, showed Lee and General Stonewall Jackson at prayer with two young children. Generally sold by mail order, these plates usually cost about $30 each.

Commemorative coins are minted from time to time. One of George Bush's last acts as president was to sign into law the Civil War Battlefield Commemorative Coin Act. It authorized the U.S. Mint to strike three coins for sale to the public. Profits went to the preservation of Civil War battlefields.

Over the years, a number of commemorative postage stamps have been issued that relate to the war—usually battlefields or personalities. Stamps can be purchased individually by sheets or as first-day covers and can be attractively mounted and framed. Most stamp dealers stock these commemoratives and first-day covers and advertise frequently in Civil War publications.

Toy soldiers, known formally as military miniatures, are available from a number of sources. They vary a lot in size, quality, and, of course, price. Miniatures can be purchased painted, mounted, and ready to be displayed, or unpainted. Or you can buy molds and make your own miniatures from scratch.

Replicas of Civil War firearms are available, some of which are beautifully made. Some gun dealers stock authentic replicas of Colt revolvers—the Third Model Dragoon, the 1860 Army Cavalry Model with fluted cylinder, and the 1861 Navy. Reenactors go into battle carrying replicas of vintage rifle-muskets or carbines. They wear replicas of Union and Confederate uniforms and carry replicas of the proper accouterments—all of which are available to collectors at shops that cater to reenactors. The better replica firearms are in the $750 to $1,500 range.

Art

A & K Historical Art, P.O. Box 6521, Hamden, CT 06517, 800-286-3084.

Americana House, Inc., 18 E. Chestnut St., Chicago, IL 60611, 312-944-3085.

American Print Gallery, P.O. Box 4477, Gettysburg, PA 17325, 800-448-1863.

Breedlove Enterprises, 1527 E. Amherst Rd., Massillon, OH 44648, 800-426-4629.

Collector Military Art, Inc., 3118 Barcelona St., Tampa, FL 33629, 813-831-9517.

Fredericksburg Historical Prints, 614 Caroline St., Fredericksburg, VA 22401, 540-373-1861.

Heron Publishing, P.O. Box 14607, Odessa, TX 79768, 800-999-0445.

Historical Art Prints, Ltd., P.O. Box 500, Southbury, CT 06488, 203-292-6680.

K & G Enterprises, P.O. Box 3778, Tucson, AZ 85722.

Martin's Gallery, 219 Steinwehr Ave., Gettysburg, PA 17325, 800-426-4659.

Virginia Fine Arts Studio, 3600 Sprucedale Dr., Annandale, VA 22023, 703-750-0025.

Miniatures and Toy Soldiers

Armchair General's Mercantile, 1008 Adans, Bay City, MI 48708, 517-892-6177.

A 12-pound Napoleon howitzer, named for the Emperor Louis Napoleon who helped develop this smoothbore field artillery piece, looks down at Chattanooga from the heights of Lookout Mountain. Napoleons were popular with both the Union and Confederate armies, but before the war ended, they were eclipsed by rifled cannons. (NPS)

Burlington Antique Toys, 1082 Madison Ave., New York, NY 10028, 212-861-9708.

Dutkins' Collectibles, 1019 Route 70, Cherry Hill, NJ 08002.

Le Petit Soldier Shop, 528 Rue Royale, New Orleans, LA 70130, 504-523-7741.

Mr. "K" Products, P.O. Box 5234, Fairlawn, OH 44334.

Saratoga Soldier, 831 Rte. 67, Ballston Spa, NY 12020, 518-885-1497

Stone Mountain, Box 584, Bloomfield, CO 80020.

Miscellaneous Collectibles

The American Historical Foundation, 1142 W. Grace St., Richmond, VA 23220, 800-368-8080. Replicas of Civil War pistols.

Dale C. Anderson Co., 4 W. Confederate Ave., Gettysburg, PA 17325. Accouterments, arms, and collectibles.

Collectors Antiquities, 60 Manor Rd., Staten Island, NY 10310. Accouterments and arms.

The Flag Center, Inc., 9 S. Harvie St., Richmond, VA 23220.

Heath & Sons, 827 S. 57th St., Springfield, OR 97478, 503-747-8169. Battlefield medallions.

Heritage Rare Coin Galleries, 311 Market St., Dallas, TX 75202. Confederate war bonds.

The Horse Soldier of Gettysburg, P.O. Box 184, Cashtown, PA 17310. General antiques and collectibles related to cavalry.

Military Collectibles, Box 971, Minden, LA 71005.

War Between the States Memorabilia, P.O. Box 3965, Gettysburg, PA 17325, 717-337-2853.

Confederate uniforms, rifles, and swords displayed in a U. S. Sanitary Commission exhibition would bring a small fortune at auction today. Confederate equipment commands much higher prices than comparable Union equipment because of its scarcity. (NA)

Appendix C
SOURCES OF
ADDITIONAL
INFORMATION

LIBRARIES AND COLLECTIONS

Alabama

Birmingham Public Library, 2020 7th Ave. N, Birmingham, AL 35203. Collection of 15,000 books, documents, and other materials.

Mobile Public Library, 701 Government St., Mobile, AL 36602. Personal papers and documents of Daniel Geary, C.S.A. Director of Mobile Defenses, 1861.

Troy State University Library, Troy, AL 36801. Papers, 25 volumes, and manuscripts of John H. Dent, noted plantation owner, covering 1851-92.

Arizona

Northern Arizona University Special Collection Library, P.O. Box 6022, Flagstaff, AZ 86011. Jo Strachan Collection.

California

California Institute of Technology Memorial Library, 1201 E. California Blvd., Pasadena, CA 91125. Collection of 3,000 volumes of Civil War material, including letters and papers of Morley and Amos G. Throop.

Claremont College Honnoid Library, 9th and Dartmouth Sts., Claremont, CA 91711. Extensive Civil War material in 70,000-volume library.

Lincoln Memorial Shrine, A. K. Smiley Public Library, 125 W. Vine St., Redlands, CA 92373. One of the largest collections of President Lincoln memorabilia, including 3,000 campaign badges, medals, pamphlets, prints, and stamps.

Occidental College Library, 1600 Campus Rd., Los Angeles, CA 90041. Manuscripts, maps, and photographs.

San Diego State University Malcolm A. Love Library, 5300 Campanile Dr., San Diego, CA 92182. Artifacts, diaries, manuscripts, and maps from Civil War period.

Stanford University Libraries, Stanford, CA 94305. Papers of Union Generals William Schafter and Frederick Steele.

University of California–San Diego Central Library, La Jolla, CA 92093. Manuscript collection and family correspondence from Civil War.

University of California–Santa Barbara Library, Santa Barbara, CA 93106. Collection of 31,000 volumes, including William Wyles Collection of Americana.

Delaware

Hagley Museum and Library, P.O. Box 3630, Greenville, DE 19807. Patent papers and papers of Union Admiral Samuel Francis du Pont and General Henry du Pont.

District of Columbia

American Red Cross National Headquarters Library, 17th and D Sts. NW, Washington, DC 20006. Clara Barton Memorial Collection and material relating to women's role in Civil War and to U.S. Sanitary Commission.

Ford Theater National Historic Site, 511 10th St. NW, Washington, DC 20004. Many Lincoln artifacts.

Georgetown University Library, 37th and O Sts. NW, Washington, DC 20057. Correspondence of various Civil War military figures and politicians.

A full suit of armor looks out of place in an exhibit of Confederate battle flags and weapons. Fascinated with the trappings of war, the folks at home flocked to such exhibitions, which raised money to provide coffee and sandwiches and other small comforts for the husbands and sons at the front. (NA)

Library of Congress, Washington, DC 20540. Papers of Union General William T. Sherman, photographs by Matthew Brady and staff, and massive Civil War print and broadside collection.

National Archives, Washington, DC. Nationwide network of presidential libraries, archive offices, and federal record centers. Emancipation Proclamation and General Robert E. Lee's 1865 signed amnesty oath.

National Museum of American History, Washington, DC 20540. Isadore Warshaw Collection of business Americana, including numerous advertising posters, flyers, and other items relating to Civil War.

Georgia

Carnegie Library, 607 Broad St., Rome, GA 30161. Collection of Civil War material, including 450 volumes and maps.

Emory University Robert W. Woodruff Library, Atlanta, GA 30322. Collection of 16,000 volumes, manuscripts, maps, and pictures.

Georgia Southern College Library, Statesboro, GA 30458. Papers of Spencer Wallace Cone.

Illinois

Chicago Historical Society Library, 1601 N. Clark St., Chicago, IL 60614. Manuscripts, maps, and 150,000 volumes, plus 27 volumes of Meserve American with 8,000 Civil War photographs.

Chicago Public Library, 78 E. Washington St., Chicago, IL 60602. Collection of 7,000 volumes. Antislavery pamphlets; many regimental histories; manuscripts of Sherman, General Ulysses S. Grant, and Confederate General John Breckinridge; letters, diaries, and photographs; C.S.A. battle plan for Shiloh; arms, equipment, and uniforms; and G.A.R. Hall and Memorial Association of Illinois Collection.

Galesburg Public Library, 40 E. Simmons St., Galesburg, IL 61401. Major Lincoln concentration and Illinois regimental histories.

Illinois State Historical Society Library, Old State Capitol, Springfield, IL 62706. Collection of 16,000 volumes, manuscripts, maps, and photographs.

The Requa Battery, one of many attempts to invent a successful machine gun, had 25 barrels mounted flat on a metal platform. It was called the "covered bridge gun" because it was designed to stop enemy charges across a covered bridge. It was capable of firing seven volleys of 175 shots a minute. (USMA)

Illinois State University Miller Library, Normal, IL 61761. Harold K. Sage Lincoln Collection of 1,200 volumes and 1,500 pamphlets, newspaper clippings, and correspondences.

Knox College Library, Galesburg, IL 61401. Collection of approximately 15,000 volumes.

Lincoln's Tomb Historic Site, Oak Ridge Cemetery, Springfield, IL 62706. Lincoln family resting place, with numerous photographs and artifacts.

McLean County Historical Society Library and Museum, 201 E. Grove St., Bloomington, IL 51701. Collection of 3,000 volumes, maps, manuscripts, and photographs, plus military heritage of Illinois, including 33rd and 94th Regiments, 3rd Volunteer Infantry.

Indiana

Butler University Irwin Library, 4600 Sunset Ave., Indianapolis, IN 46208. Charles W. Moore Lincoln Collection.

Indiana University Lily Library, 7th St., Bloomington, IN 47405. Collection of 160,000 volumes, including manuscripts, maps, and photographs.

Louis A. Warren Lincoln Library and Museum, Ft. Wayne, IN 46602. Significant collection of Lincoln photography.

Morrison-Reeves Library, 80 N. 6th St., Richmond, IN 47474. Extensive collection on Civil War and Lincoln.

Willard Library, 21 1st Ave., Evansville, IN 47710. Collection of 500 volumes, including battle accounts, biographies of generals, diaries, letters, and memoirs.

Iowa

State Historical Society of Iowa Library, 402 Iowa Ave., Iowa City, IA 52240. Iowa regimental histories, diaries, and similar materials.

Kentucky

Abraham Lincoln Birthplace National Historic Site, Rte. 1, Hodgenville, KY 42748. Reconstructed log cabin furnished with Lincoln artifacts.

Louisiana

Louisiana State University Troy H. Middleton Library, Baton Rouge, LA 70803. Warren Jones Lincoln Collection.

Tulane University Howard–Tilton Memorial Library, 7001 Feret St., New Orleans, LA 70118. Diaries, letters of Louisiana soldiers, and papers of Lee, General P. T. G. Beauregard, T. J. Jackson, A. S. Johnson, and J. H. Stubbs.

Maine

Bowdoin College Library, Brunswick, ME 04011. Military papers, including Chamberlain and Fessenden family materials and Oliver Otis, Hubbard, and McArthur family papers, most of which pertain to Civil War.

Maine Historical Society Library, 485 Congress St., Portland, ME 14101. Extensive collection on Maine regiments.

Maryland

Antietam National Battlefield Site Library, P.O. Box 158, Sharpsburg, MD 21782. Monographs on regiments and troopers.

Hood College Joseph Henry Apple Library, Rosemont Ave., Frederick, MD 21701. Irving M. Landauer Civil War Collection.

Salisbury State College Blackwell Library, Salisbury, MD 21801. Extensive collection of Civil War material.

Massachusetts

American Antiquarian Society, 185 Salisbury St., Worcester, MA 01609. Vast ephemeral printing collection, much of it Civil War-related.

Boston University Muger Memorial Library, 771 Commonwealth Ave., Boston, MA 02215. Paul Richard Collection.

Concord Free Public Library, 129 Main St., Concord, MA 01741. Manuscripts, maps, and photographs.

Harvard University Widener Library, Cambridge, MA 02138.

Lynn Public Library, 5 N. Common St., Lynn, MA 01902. Papers and books relating to Massachusetts regiments.

Memorial Hall Library, Elm St., Andover, MA 01810. Charles Barry original drawings of Lincoln.

State Library of Massachusetts, 341 State St., Boston, MA 02133. Extensive collection on New England's participation in Civil War.

Michigan

Andrews University James White Library, Berrian Springs, MI 49104. Courville Collection of some 350 items, including accessories, weaponry, and more.

University of Michigan William L. Clements Library, Ann Arbor, MI 48109. Vast collection of Civil War-related material.

Mississippi

University of Southern Mississippi William D. McCain Graduate Library, P.O. Box 5148, Southern Station, MS 39406. Ernest A. Walen Collection relating to history of C.S.A., including more than 600 Confederate imprints, various manuscripts, and collections.

Missouri

Central Missouri State University Ward Edwards Library, Warrensburg, MO 64093. Extensive border-state material.

Montana

Eastern Montana State College Library, 1500 N. 30th St., Billings, MT 59101. General George Armstrong Custer's personal and military papers, complete 7th Cavalry records, and numerous Civil War papers from Custer Battlefield National Monument Collection.

New Hampshire

New Hampshire Historical Society Manuscripts Library, 30 Park St., Concord, NH 03301. Military records of New Hampshire regiments.

During the Civil War period, photographers were learning how to manipulate images. Here George Washington seems to have descended from heaven to embrace President Lincoln and, by extension, his conduct of the war. Prints like these were sold at stationers and general stores. (GG)

New Jersey

Princeton University Library, Nassau St., Princeton, NJ 08540. James Perkins Walker Collection, including Civil War papers.

New York

Buffalo and Erie Historical Society, 25 Nottingham Ct., Buffalo, NY 14216. Major collection of Civil War military history.

Columbia University Libraries, 801 Butler Library, 535 W. 114th St., New York, NY 10027. Papers of Allan Nevins, Sydney H. Gray, and Peter A. Alexander.

Fenton Historical Society Library, 67 Washington, Jamestown, NY 14701. Collection of diaries, letters, muster rolls, history of New York state regiments, and other items.

New York Historical Society Library, 170 Central Park West, New York, NY 10024. Extensive ephemera holdings, including Bella C. Landauer Collection.

New York Public Library, 5th Ave. and 42nd St., New York, NY 10016. Collection of 25,000 volumes.

St. John Fisher College Library, Rochester, NY 14627. Collection of more than 1,000 volumes, including papers and records of G.A.R.

St. Lawrence University Owen D. Young Library, Canton, NY 13617. Correspondence from numerous Union volunteers and papers of Union spy Pryce Lewis.

Union League Club Library, 38 E. 37th St., New York, NY 10018. Collection of 30,000 volumes.

University Club Library, 1 W. 54th St., New York, NY 10016. Southern Society Collection of papers and memorabilia on C.S.A. and Reconstruction.

U.S. Military Academy Library, West Point, NY 10996. Extensive collection of battle accounts (USMA graduates were 37 percent of C.S.A.'s 425 generals and 40 percent of Union's 583 generals).

North Carolina

Duke University William R. Perkins Library, Durham, NC 27706. Papers of Lee and Beauregard, C.S.A. government, and Confederate President Jefferson Davis, as well as thousands of Union and C.S.A.diaries and letters.

University of North Carolina-Chapel Hill Wilson Library, Chapel Hill, NC 28514.Wilmer Collection of more than 825 Civil War novels, from 1861 to present, with related bibliographical material.

Ohio

Ohio Historical Society, Archives Library Division, 1982 Velma Ave., Columbus, OH 43211. Regimental histories and Ohio war narratives.

Ohio University Vernon R. Alden Library, Athens, OH 45701. Brown family papers covering activities of 36th Ohio and 4th West Virginia Regiments and Kentucky campaign.

Public Library of Cincinnati and Hamilton County, 800 Vine St., Cincinnati, OH 45202. Collection focusing on Ohio military unit histories.

Western Reserve Historical Society Library, 10825 East Blvd., Cleveland, OH 44106.William P. Palmer Civil War Collection.

Wilmington College Watson Library, P.O. Box 1227, Wilmington, OH 45177. Collection focusing on Ohio Quakers and their role during Civil War.

Pennsylvania

Adams County Historical Society, Gettysburg, PA 17325. Extensive collection of manuscripts, maps, and photographs.

Gettysburg College Musselman Library, Gettysburg, PA 17325. Documents and artifacts from area battlegrounds.

Gettysburg National Military Park, Gettysburg, PA 17325.Vast collection of 18,000 photographs and other materials on Battle of Gettysburg and other campaigns.

Military Order of the Loyal Legion of the U.S. War Library and Museum, 1805 Pine St., Philadelphia, PA 19103. Collection of 10,000 volumes.

Pontoon bridges erected by Union engineers allowed the rapid transport of men and equipment across water barriers. At Fredericksburg in 1862, they provided the only avenue of attack for federal troops. In 1864, Union engineers built a 2,200-foot span in just three hours, enabling Grant to cross the James ahead of Lee. (LC)

Union League of Philadelphia Library, 140 S. Broad St., Philadelphia, PA 19102. Significant Civil War collection, including papers of Union Secretary of War Edwin Stanton, with fascinating commentary on Lincoln's assassination.

University of Pittsburgh Hillman Library, Pittsburgh, PA 15260. Collection of 10,000 volumes, including collections of Eli H. Canfield, William Corliss, Elmer Ellsworth, Rush C. Hawkins, John Hay, and Augustus Woodbury and McClellan-Lincoln Collection (partial, see also "Rhode Island, Brown University").

U.S. Army Military Institute, Carlisle Barracks, Carlisle, PA 17013. Large collection of personal diaries, letters, and memoirs of Union and C.S.A. military.

Rhode Island

Brown University John Hay Library, 20 Prospect St., Providence, RI 02912. Part of McClellan-Lincoln Collection, which is one of the most esteemed Lincoln holdings, acquired for Brown by John D. Rockerfeller (see also "Pennsylvania, University of Pittsburgh"). Collection of some 15,000 volumes and much related material.

Providence Public Library, 150 Empire St., Providence, RI 02903. Harris Collection of slavery and Civil War regimental histories, accounts of war by women, and writings of abolitionists.

South Carolina

College of Charleston Library, Charleston, SC 29401. Wartime records from Bank of Charleston as well as personal letters and papers of area families.

South Carolina Historical Society Library, 100 Meeting St., Charleston, SC 29401. Collection of 50,000 volumes relating to South Carolina's pivotal role in secession and Civil War.

University of South Carolina Library, Columbia, SC 29208. Reputedly, the South's richest collection, strong in regimental histories of both C.S.A. and Union.

Few cavalry leaders on either side could compare with confederate Colonel John S. Mosby. Operating an independent command in Virginia, he was so successful that Grant ordered him hanged with trial, if captured. Wounded seven times but never captured, Mosby estimated that his activities kept at least 30,000 Union soldiers away from the front. (NA)

Tennessee

Lincoln Memorial University Carnegie Library, Harrogate, TN 37752. Within Abraham Lincoln Center for Lincoln Studies, one of the nation's largest Lincoln and Civil War collections, including material from National Civil War Council Center regarding military surgery and medicine. Also, within Center for Study of Military Music, 7,000 sheet music entries.

Memphis Pink Palace Museum Library, 3050 Central Ave., Memphis TN 38111. Numerous items on loan from Shiloh Military Trail, Inc., and other sources.

Public Library of Nashville and Davidson County, 8th Ave. N at Union St., Nashville, TN 37203. Collection of material on area battles and area wartime personalities.

University of Tennessee–Chattanooga Library, Chattanooga, TN 37401. Collection of 3,500 volumes.

Texas

Rice University Fondren Library, 6100 S. Main St., P.O. Box 1892, Houston, TX 77251. Several collections of diaries, letters, and military records.

Sam Houston State University Library, P.O. Box 2179, Huntsville, TX 77340. Porter Confederate Collection on role of Texas in Civil War.

University of Texas Libraries, P.O. Box P, Austin, TX 78713. Littlefield Collection of research materials, including many rare items on history of antebellum South.

Virginia

George C. Marshall Research Foundation and Library, Drawer 920, Lexington, VA 24450. William F. Friedman Collection, featuring Civil War code items.

Petersburg National Battlefield Library, Box 549, Petersburg, VA 23804. Detailed information on various engagements during siege of Petersburg.

Portsmouth Public Library, 601 Court St., Portsmouth, VA 23704. Special collection of Tidewater and Lower Tidewater history.

University of Virginia Alderman Library, Charlottesville, VA 22901. About 1,500 collections containing materials related to Civil War, particularly Army of Northern Virginia and campaigns and battles in Virginia. Diaries, letters, reminiscences, maps, and pictorial material of Confederate soldiers and civilians; and papers of Lee, General J. E. B. Stuart, Thomas L. Rosser, Jubal Early, John Daniel Imboden, William "Extra Billy" Smith, Henry Alexander Wise, Eppa Hunton, John S. Mosby, and Samuel Barron.

Virginia State Library, 12th and Capital Sts., Richmond, VA 23319. Collection of vast amount of pictorial material.

Washington and Lee University Library, Lexington, VA 24450. Collection of 25,000 volumes and 10,000 manuscripts emphasizing Lee's life, Virginia, and Civil War, as well as 8,000 glass-plate photographs by Miley.

Wisconsin

State Historical Society of Wisconsin Archives, 816 State St., Madison, WI 53706. Collection focusing on Wisconsin's part in Civil War.

University of Wisconsin–Madison Memorial Library, 728 State St., Madison, WI 53706. Rare collection of manuscripts of military brass band that marched with Sherman's army.

University of Wisconsin–Milwaukee Library, 3203 N. Denver St., Milwaukee, WI 53201. Allen M. Slichter Collection of Confederate war material.

ORGANIZATIONS

Armies of Tennessee (C.S.A. and U.S.A.), P.O. Box 91, Rosedale, IN 47874.

Association for the Preservation of Civil War Sites, Inc. (APCWS), P.O. Box 162, Fredericksburg, VA 22402.

Children of the Confederacy, P.O. Box 4868, Richmond, VA 23220.

Civil War Press Corps, P.O. Box 856, Colonial Heights, VA 23834.

Civil War Round Table Association, P.O. Box 7388, Little Rock, AR 72217.

Confederate Historical Institute, P.O. Box 7388, Little Rock, AR 72217.

Confederate Memorial Literary Society, The Museum of the Confederacy, 1201 E. Clay St., Richmond, VA 23221.

Daughters of Union Veterans, 403 S. Walnut St., Springfield, IL 62704.

Hood's Texas Brigade Association, Hill College History Complex, P.O. Box 619, Hillsboro, TX 76645.

Institute of Civil War Studies, International Institute for Advanced Studies, Suite 403, 8000 Bonhomme St., Clayton, MO 63105.

Jefferson Davis Association, P.O. Box 1892, Rice University, Houston, TX 77251.

Ladies of the GAR, Elizabeth B. Koch, 204 E. Sellers Ave., Ridley Park, PA 19078.

Military Order of the Loyal Legion, 1805 Pine St., Philadelphia, PA 19103.

Military Order of the Stars and Bars, P.O. Box 5164, Southern Station, Hattiesburg, PA 19103.

Military Order of the Zouave Legion, 513 Greynolds Cir., Lantana, FL 33462.

National Society of Andersonville, P.O. Box 65, Andersonville, GA 31711.

National Woman's Relief Corps, 629 S. 7th St., Springfield, IL 62703.

Robert E. Lee Memorial Association, Stratford Hall Plantation, Stratford, VA 22558.

Sam Davis Memorial Association, P.O. Box 1, Smyrna, TN 37167.

Sons of Confederate Veterans, P.O. Box 5164, Hattiesburg, MS 39401.

Sons of Sherman's March, 1725 Farmer Ave., Tempe, AZ 85281.

Sons of Union Veterans, 200 Washington St., Suite 614, Wilmington, DE 19801.

Ulysses S. Grant Association, Morris Library, Southern Illinois University, Carbondale, IL 62901.

United Daughters of the Confederacy, P.O. Box 4868, Richmond, VA 23220.

PERIODICALS

For Civil War Enthusiasts

Artilleryman, Cutter & Locke, Inc., 4 Water St., P.O. Box C, Arlington, MA 02174. Published quarterly.

Blue & Gray Magazine, Blue & Gray Enterprises, Inc., P.O. Box 28685, Columbus, OH 43228. Published monthly.

Camp Chase Gazette, 3984 Cincinnati-Zanesville Rd. NE, Lancaster, OH 43130. Covers upcoming Civil War commemorative events and reenactments. Published 10 times a year.

Civil War Magazine, Civil War Society Country Publishers, Inc., 133 E. Main St., P.O. Box C, Arlington, MA 02174. Published bimonthly.

Civil War News, P.O. Box C, Arlington, MA 02174. Newspaper. Published 9 times a year.

Civil War Times Illustrated, Cowles Magazines, 2245 Kohn Rd., P.O. Box 8200, Harrisburg, PA 17105-8200. Largest in field, with 160,000 readers. Published monthly.

Confederate Veteran, Sons of Confederate Veterans, P.O. Box 820169, Houston, TX 77282-0169. Nonmembers may subscribe. Published bimonthly.

Grave Matters, 1163 Warrenhall Ln., Atlanta, GA 30319. Newsletter for necrolithographers and those in quest of Civil War battlegrounds.

Journal of Confederate History, Guild Bindery Press, P.O. Box 2071, Lakeway Station, Paris, TN 37752-0901. Book-length publication. Published quarterly.

Lincoln Herald, Lincoln Memorial University Press, Harrogate, TN 37752-0901. Published quarterly.

Southern Partisan, Southern Heritage Society, P.O. Box 11708, Charleston, SC 29211. Membership includes magazine and quarterly newsletter. Published quarterly.

Union Times, 7214 Laurel Hill Rd., Orlando, FL 32818. Covers upcoming Civil War commemorative events and reenactments. Published 8 times a year.

Somewhere in Virginia, a private stands at attention as officers of the 1st New York Infantry pose for a photographer in front of the Stars and Stripes and regimental flag. Neither their slouch hats nor the private's kepi offered protection in battle, but helmets were still several wars away. (NA)

For Collectors

Antiques Review, 12 E. Stafford, Worthington, OH 43085. Tabloid newspaper covering major shows and auctions, but including those with toys, Americana, and Civil War-related items. Published monthly.

Antique Toy World, P.O. Box 34509, Chicago, IL 60634. Published monthly.

Civil War Book Exchange & Collector's Newspaper, Cutter & Locke, Inc., 4 Water St., P.O. Box C, Arlington, MA 02174. Published 6 times a year.

The Courier, P.O. Box 1863, Williamsville, NY 14221.

Guide to Buyers, Sellers, & Traders of Black Collectibles, CGL, Box 158472, Nashville, TN 37215. Newsletter. Published monthly.

Keynoter, P.O. Box 340339, San Antonio, TX 78234. Official American Political Items Collector publication, issued as part of membership. Published 3 times a year.

CIVIL WAR AUCTIONS ON THE INTERNET

The Internet has become increasingly useful to collectors of Civil War antiques. **Miles of History (online auction; http://www.collectorsnet. con/miles)** sells Civil War memorabilia, including documents, photographs, weapons, uniform buttons, and insignia, by auction on the Internet. Civil War items also turn up on auctions conducted by **Antiquephoto.com (http:// www.antiquephoto.com)**, **Philatelists Online (http://www. antiquephoto.com)**, and the **Annex Galleries (http://www.cais.net/ auction)**.

Most on-line auctions follow standard auction house procedures (and beware of those that don't). The typical guidelines for on-line auction houses are similar to what you may expect from a good reputable auction house. All artifacts are guaranteed authentic and come with a five-day inspection privilege. Any item varying significantly can be returned with a written

The mainstay of the Union coastal defense was the Columbiad, a smoothbore gun capable of firing both shot and shell at a high angle of elevation. The gun was invented in 1811 and could fire 225-pound bolts 1,100 to 1,800 yards. Most Columbiads were of 8- or 10-inch caliber. The Confederacy also fabricated Columbiads. (LC)

explanation providing it is in the same condition it was in when received. There is a 10 percent buyer's premium, and the buyer pays for shipping and insurance. Minimum bid an on any lot is $10 or 40 percent of the estimated value, whichever is greater. Bids must be in whole dollars and cannot be "buy bids," —that is, "better than all other bids to acquire this item." Successful bidders will be invoiced within 5 business days. Payment must be received within 10 days. After 10 days a late payment fee of $25 will be assessed. Bids can be may be made by mail, phone, or E-mail. In case of tie bids, the earliest one received prevails.

A collector also can use the Internet to get information on regular auctions. **The Auction Hunters (http://www.auctionhunter.com)** is a searchable data base of antiques, collectibles, real estate, and fine art auctions in the Northeast. The **Internet Auction List (http://www.usaweb.com/auction.htm)** is another source, listing hundreds of auctioneers' sites by category, as well as national publications that include auction schedules.

The amount of information on the Internet about the war is nearly overwhelming. A recent check by the author found 24 category and 474 site matches for the search phrase "civil war." Sites include Civil War computer games; state, regional, and regimental histories; specific battles; rosters of combatants; public and personal documents; biographies of Civil War personalities; Civil War round-table discussions; news about reenactments and reenactors; news and articles from Civil War magazines; and a wealth of images—Matthew Brady collection from the Library of Congress, photographs from the Museum of the Confederacy, maps, and images of battle flags.

Of course, there are gaps, but the number of things available grows by leaps and bounds, and probably will continue to do so.

A photograph of a young boy pretending to be a soldier was a reminder of home to his father away serving in the army. Photography thrived in the Civil War. It was an exciting new novelty, and people flocked to professional photographic studios to have their pictures taken. (GG)

Appendix D

A GUIDE TO PRICES

C ivil War antiques, like all antiques, are unique; no two are exactly the same. Even mass-produced items, such as firearms and accouterments and army manuals, vary in condition, and condition is an important factor in determining the price of an item. For that reason, this guide can report only the range of prices that similar items have commanded in the recent past, or what one such item fetched at auction. Prices have risen slowly but steadily over the years, and within the past decade, prices of Confederate items have increased considerably more than the prices of comparable Federal items. Beyond these caveats, remember that these prices are only guides and that there is no substitute for the advice of a knowledgeable collector or reputable dealer.

ACCOUTERMENTS

Plates

Accouterment plates are popular with collectors, and rare Confederate plates command very high prices. Unfortunately for the collector, many plates have been reproduced and some have been passed off as originals. Expert advice is recommended, particularly if the collector is not buying from a well-established dealer or at auction.

The designations "E" and "NE" refer to relics that are excavated or nonexcavated. Excavated relics are those that are recovered from battlefields, usually with the help of a metal detector. Excavated relics, therefore, have been carried in battle. For this reason, they command higher prices from collectors, although their condition is invariably poorer than that of non-excavated relics.

Oval US cartridge-box plate, oval, large	$95E, $85NE
US belt plate, oval, large	$140E or NE
Ornate two-piece US naval sword belt plate	$300E, $225NE
Maine, small oval VMM belt plate.	$475E, $450NE
New York cast-brass SNY sword breast plate	$450E, $400NE
Pennsylvania, large oval state-seal plate	$2,200E, $1,800NE
CS standard tongue-in-wreath sword belt plate	$3,250E, $3,150NE
CS oval, regulation style	$2,100E, $2,500NE
CS oval, solid cast, surrounded by 11 stars	$7,250E, $8,150NE
Alabama oval state-seal waist belt plate	$5,500E, $6,000NE
Georgia oval militia (GM) plate	$3,000E, $2,900NE
Virginia, round state-seal cross belt plate	$4,700E, $5,200NE
Frame buckle, common Confederate cast	$450E, $525NE
Frame buckle, cavalry frame	$500E, $575NE
Frame buckle, Western-style, U-tongue	$900E, $975NE
Carbine sling belt buckle, marked	$95E, $100NE
Drummer's sling buckle	$350E, $325NE

ADVERTISING EPHEMERA

Signs

"'Goodbye, God Spare You' Soldier's Farewell." Ca. 1860s.
Cincinnati, Hamilton & Dayton Railway. 17 X 11½" embossed
sign of departing soldier being embraced by sweetheart.
Inset of small map of railway $200 to $225

"A Proclamation by Abraham Lincoln: 75,000 Men Wanted.
Enlist Under One Captain." Ca. 1870s. Takeoff on recruiting
broadside but actually advertising Massabesic House, a
lake resort in New Hampshire $125 to $150

"Stonewall Jackson Cigars." Stand-up embossed tin sign
multicolor, 9 X 11½." Shaped like a cigar box, Jackson's
portrait on lid $300 to $400

Trade Cards

"Jefferson Davis—The Glorious and Inglorious Career
in Five Expressive Tableaus." Mechanical trade card.
1861. Satirical mix and match with different tops
and bottoms $150 to $200

"S.R. Fondren, Auctioneer for Sale of Negroes."
Richmond, Va. 1850s. 3½ X 2½" $250 to $350

(Gen. U.S. Grant) "The Boss Puzzle." 1872. Roscoe Conkling
agonizes over maneuvering wooden game pieces represented
by heads of various presidential candidates, including Grant,
Sherman, Blaine, Tilden, etc. $35 to $45

(Gen. Philip Sheridan) Clark Threads. Ca. 1894. Donaldson
Bros., Five Points, NY. Three vignettes of Sheridan: portrait,
on famous ride, and two horseman with sabers $20 to $25

ARTILLERY

Cannons

Few collectors have the space or the money to collect Civil War cannons. And cannons are hard to come by. Experts estimate that there are nearly 5,000 surviving muzzlel-loading cannons, but most of them are in national or state parks or are on monuments. Only a few hundred are privately owned. Cannons are sold so infrequently as to make setting an average price difficult. There are two basic categories of cannons—iron and bronze. Bronze cannons are more desirable and thus more expensive than iron. Confederate cannons are rarer and command higher prices than Federal cannons.

Iron Cannons

3-inch Parrot rifle	$18,000 to 22,000
CSA Parrott rifle	$30,000 and up
CSA Noble Bros. 3-inch rifle	$27,000 and up
CSA Tredegar 12-pdr. howitzer	$30,000 and up

Bronze Cannons

12-pdr. Model 1841 field howitzer	$24,00 to $26,000
12-pdr. Model 1857 Napoleon	$35,000 to $40,000
14-pdr. Model 1861 James rifle	$32,000 to $36,000
24-pdr. Model 1838 Coehorn mortar	$6,000 to $8,000
12-pdr. CSA Napoleon	$50,000 and up

Equipment

Gunner's calipers	$300 to $400
Gunner's quadrant, brass	$700 and up
Gunner's level	$600 and up
Gunner's haversack	$400 and up
Fuse reamer	$100 to $150
Lanyard	$50 to $100
Metal friction primer box	$150 to $200
Artillery valise saddle	$550 and up

At the Pea Ridge National Battlefield in Arkansas, a 3-inch rifled cannon still stands guard. Some 1,000 Cherokees from the Indian Nation (now Oklahoma) fought with the rebels and charged cannons like this one, which they called "shooting wagons." (CT)

Field artillery, like the Pennsylvania Ringold Battery, above, was light and mobile enough to move with the army in the field, and to be freely maneuvered in battle. The workhorse of the field artillery in the war was the 12-pound smoothbore "Napoleon," Model 1847, which fired a variety of projectiles, including the anti-personnel grape shot. (NA)

US artillery limber chest	$1,700 and up
CS artillery limber chest	$3,500 and up

Fuses

Boxer self-igniting fuse, wood body, dug	$75 to $150
Britten time fuse, brass	$50 to $75
Confederate fuse plug, copper	$100 to $125
Hotchkiss fuse plug, zinc	$50 to $75
Parrott fuse plug, zinc	$25 to $50
Britten percussion fuse, brass	$125 to $200
Confederate percussion fuse, brass	$125 to $175
Sawyer percussion fuse, brass and iron, complete	$100 to $150

Tice percussion fuse, brass	$275 to $350
CS percussion fuse	$200 to $250
Navy Hotchkiss, percussion fuse, brass	$100 to $125
Rains pressure-sensitive land mine fuse, complete	$500 and up

Grenades and Rockets

Ketchum hand grenade, US 1 pdr.	$400E, $750NE
CS spherical hand grenade, 1 pdr.	$600E, $900NE
Hale rocket, US, 5 lbs., 14 oz.	$900E, $1,200NE
CS Raines land mine, 24-pdr. shell with fuse	$1,500E, $1,800NE

Shells

CS spherical, round cavity, 12-pdr., 4.62 in.	$100 to $150
US spherical, Bormann fuse, 24-pdr., 5.82 in.	$90 to $130
US Hotchkiss, 4.62-in. canister	$650 and up
CS Archer, round nose, 3-in. rifle, 809 lbs.	$575 to $750
GB Britten, 3-in. rifle shell, 6 lbs.	$550 to $750
CS Brooke, short body, 3-in. rifle, 9 lbs., "G"	$600 to $750
US Ellsworth, round nose, 6-pdr. rifle, 506 lbs.	$300 to $400
US James, Type I, hollow base, 6-pdr., 12 lbs.	$300 to $400
US Parrott, flat top, 10-pdr. rifle, 9 to 10 lbs.	$200 to $275
CS Read, smooth body, pointed nose, 10-pdr., 12 lbs.	$250 to $325
US Sawyer, lead sabot, 15 to 16 lbs.	$200 to $350
US Schenkl, rounded nose, 2-in. rifle, 7 to 8 lbs.	$250 to $375
GB Whitworth, hexagonal sides, 6-pdr., 11 to 12 lbs.	$650 to $850
USN Cochran, variant, 80-pdr. rifle, 60 lbs.	$1,000 and up
USN Dahlgren, variant, 30-pdr. rifle, blind shell, 38 lbs.	$300 to $550

BAYONETS

Angular or Socket Bayonets

US rifle-musket 1855-70.	$75 to $100
US rifle M-1841 (Mississippi)	$150 to $250
US Spencer rifle M-1860	$100 to $150
CS Richmond rifle-musket	$500 to $750
CS Fayetteville rifle	$650 to $850
British Enfield rifle-musket M-1853	$70 to $90
Austrian Lorenz, .54 cal.	$70 to $90

Sword-Saber Bayonets

US musketoon M-1847	$1,000 to $1,500
Sharps rifle M-1860	$200 to $275
Henry rifle	$1,000 and up
CS Boyle, Gamble & McFee, marked	$2,000 and up
CS Cook & Brother rifle	$1,300 and up
Unknown Confederate	$500 to $900
British Navy rifle	$225 to $350
Lancaster English rifle	$200 to $300

BROADSIDES, PRINTS, POSTERS, AND MAPS

"$100,000 Reward/War Dept. April 20, 1865. The murderer
of our late beloved President, Abraham Lincoln is still at large."
Descriptions of Booth, Surratt, and Herold $9,000 to $10,000

"Another Chance! To Avoid the Draft. Enlist in the 7th
Indiana Cavalry." P.C. Shanks, Indianapolis, poster.
Large eagle with legend in talons: "$400 dollars
bounty" $1,200 to $1,400

California Recruiting. Ca. 1863-64. "$100 bounty! 50 men
Wanted for Company L., 1st Cavalry, Cal. Vols!/For Active
Service in Texas/Apply at . . . James, Gorman."
Large woodcut eagle illustration and black border.
23 X 16½" $1,800 to $2,000

George Armstrong Custer, Congratulatory Order,
Appomattox Issued by Custer praising the 3rd Cavalry.
5 X 9" $1,100 to $1,200

Gen. James Shield Irish Brigade Recruiting. Ca. 1861-62.
"2nd Regt. to Be Raised in Philadelphia/Now is the time for
Irishmen to get arms in their hands . . . " $2,500 to $3,000

"John Brown, Leader of the Harpers Ferry Insurrection."
Print. Currier & Ives, N.Y. 1870. Portrait with vignettes.
Hand-colored $100 to $125

"Storming Fort Wagner." Print. 1890. Chromolith
by Kurz & Allison, Chicago. 22 X 28" $900 to $1,000

"Confederate Camp." Print. Ca. 1865. M & N Hanhart
chromolith. 10⅝ X 15¼" $450 to $500

"Jefferson Davis and His Generals." Print. Ca. 1861.
Pub. by Goupil et Cie, Paris and Michael Knoedler,
N.Y.C. $700 to $800

Gen. U.S. Grant/1844 Print. Currier & Ives, N.Y.,
Half-length portrait $100 to $125

BULLETS

There were at least 700 varieties of bullets used in the Civil War, and most specimens of most varieties can be purchased for less then $10. Only a rare few command a price of $100 or more. The price of a bullet varies with the rarity of the firearm for which it was made. The prices listed here are for excavated bullets in good to excellent condition.

US or CS minie	$1 to $2
Picket type for country rifle, .40 cal.	$5 to $7
Unknown carbine, .52 cal.	$2 to $2
Sharps carbine, .577 cal.	$8 to $10
Colt army revolver, .44 cal.	$3 to $4
US Savage Navy revolver, .36 cal.	$30 to $40
Italian Garibaldi, .58 cal.	$20 to $35
Enfield, variant, .54 cal.	$4 to $5
Enfield explosive bullet, .58 cal.	$1 to $2
CS Whitworth cylindrical, .45 cal.	$70 to $100
CS Mississippi rifle, .54 cal.	$60 to $80
CS LeMat revolver, .42 cal.	$20 to $25
Austrian rifled musket, .71 cal.	$20 to $25

BULLET MOLDS

Brass

Mold for .36 picket bullet	$30 to $60
Mold for .36 Colt revolver	$75 to $100
Mold for .57 Enfield	$150 to $200
Mold for cylindrical, long Whitworth bullet	$475 and up

Iron

Mold for Colt .44 revolver, marked Colt	$60 to $90
Mold for Maynard carbine	$150 to $175
Gang mold for seven .69 balls	$335 and up

BUTTONS

State Seals

Alabama, various versions	$350 to $500
Arkansas, various versions	$1,700 to $3,250
Connecticut, various versions	$50 to $350
Florida various versions	$1,000 to $2,500
Georgia, various versions	$75 to $1100
Kentucky	$300 to $500
Louisiana, various versions	$125 to $1,800
Maine, various versions	$55 to $225
Maryland, various versions	$100 to $200
Massachusetts, various versions	$25 to $150
Michigan, various versions	$15 to $125
Mississippi, various versions	$150 to $550
New Hampshire, various versions	$75 to $275
New Jersey, various versions	$35 to $300
New York, various versions	$5 to $550
North Carolina, various versions	$35 to $1,000
Pennsylvania, various versions	$50 to $175
Rhode Island, various versions	$25 to $100
South Carolina, various versions	$50 to $750
Tennessee	$1,300 to $2,700
Texas, various versions	$750 to $1,750
Vermont, various versions	$30 to $150
Virginia, various versions	$75 to $1,000
Wisconsin	$75 to $100

Confederate

Officer, eagle device with CSA on shield, 11 six-point stars, two-piece with border	$750 and up
Officer, eagle device on a lined field, 12 five-point stars, two-piece with flat border	$350 to $850

General officer, 13 five-point stars encircling, two stars at bottom	$1,000 and up
Navy, anchor and crossed cannons device on a lined field, with rope border "CSN" below	$600 and up
Artillery, two-piece with border, lined Roman	$150 to $200
Artillery, two-piece with flat border, lined Old English "A"	$200 to $375
Cavalry, two-piece with border, lined Roman "C"	$125 to $275
Cavalry, two-piece with a Roman "C" and Confederate local	$200 to $400
Cavalry, flag with "CSA" above, crossed sabers below and a Confederate local	$2,000 to $3,500
Engineers, two-piece with border, Old German "E"	$115 to $275
Engineers, two-piece with border, Old English "E" and a Confederate local	$3,000 and up
Infantry, two-piece with border, lined roman "I"	$50 to $200
Infantry, two-piece with border and stippled Old German text "I"	$175 to $275
Rifleman, two piece with border	$400 to $600
Rifleman, two-piece with border, lined Old English "R"	$600 to $1,200

Federal

Artillery, two-piece eagle "A"	$15 to $25
Cavalry, high convex eagle "C"	$15 to $30
Dragoons, two-piece eagle "D"	$50 to $100
Engineers, two-piece with eagle	$50 to $100
Infantry, two-piece eagle "I"	$10 to $15
Infantry, hard-rubber eagle "I"	$75 to $150
Navy, two-piece eagle, upright anchor	$25 to $40
Navy, hard-rubber, upright anchor	$40 to $60

CAMP GEAR

Officer's camp bed, hand-wrought with wire stretched on frame with ID	$1,000 and up
Officer's camp bed, same as above but no ID	$750 to $900
Camp stool, folding, three- or four-legged, with ID	$300 to $475
Camp chest, large, wood construction, painted with ID	$550 to $950
Camp chest, same as above but without ID	$300 to $600
Field desk, with ID	$500 to $950
Field desk, without ID	$200 to $450
Camp lantern, folding, of tin, glass, or mica	$150 to $300
Hatchet, contract and US marked	$200 to $350

CANTEENS

Confederate

Tin drum style, one side flat, one convex, with sling	$550 to $750
Militia-type drum canteen	$200 to $350
Pocket-size tin drum canteen	$100 to $175
Wood-drum style with carved soldier's name and regiment	$2,500 to $3,750

Federal

Model 1858 with sling and cover	$300 to $375
Oblate spheroid canteen with tin spout	$175 to $250
Oblate spheroid canteen, Bullseye Pattern	$300 to $400
Case pattern filter model	$400 to $550
Gutta-percha model	$700 to $850

Enlisted men of Company K, 38th North Carolina Infantry, are inspected before taking part in the reenactment of the Battle of Gettysburg. Ahead of them: the fateful charge toward "the little clump of trees," the highwater mark of the Confederacy. (CT)

CAP BOXES

Federal

General issue, no markings or maker's markings, with lambs wool and vent pick intact	$75 to $150
Same as above but with small "US" die-stamped in flap	$100 to $150
Enfield pattern	$125 to $225
Navy, same as infantry but with USN on flap	$100 to $225

Confederate

General issue, one belt loop, lambs wool, vent pick	$450 and up
Marked Selma Arsenal, single belt loop	$2,000 to $3,000
Canvas, marked "N" Crown & Co., Columbus, Ga.	$2,500 to $3,500

CARTRIDGE BOXES
Federal
Standard .58-cal. M–1865, with shoulder strip, tins,
eagle plate, box plate $500 to $850

.69 cal. musket box $350 to $450

Embossed box, either .58 or .68 caliber $500 to $850

Complete Spencer rifle cartridge box $250 to $400

Mississippi rifle box $300 to $450

Standard carbine box with wood block for various
carbines $150 to $250

Confederate
General issue, no markings, for belt or
over-the-shoulder $800 and up

General issue, no markings, tarred linen with sling $2,250 to $3,500

Embossed with "CS" in oval cartouche $3,500 to $5,500

Pistol Boxes
Union, .44-cal. Colt Army pistol box $75 to $125

Union, .36-cal. Colt Navy pistol box $150 to $30

Confederate, general issue, no markings $800 to $1,400

Fuse Pouches
Union, artillery fuse pouch $125 to $250

Confederate, artillery fuse pouch, no markings $900 to $1,500

Confederate, fuse box marked "P. Darrah,
Augusta, Ga." $2,000 to $3,500

CARTRIDGES

Cartridges, like bullets, came in a great number of types and sizes to accommodate the array of Civil War firearms. Cartridges, like bullets, are inexpensive; all but a few are priced under $50.

Federal, paper, for rifle, .54, .58, or .69 cal.	$15 to $30
Federal, paper, Sharps carbine, .52 carbine	$35 to $60
Federal, paper, swagged bullet for Springfield, .58 cal.	$15 to $30
Federal, paper, for Whitworth, hexagonal bullet, cal. 45.	$125 to $150
CSA, paper, Sharps 1821, cal. 54.	$55 to $80
CS, paper, Gardner inserted, .577 cal.	$300 to $500

CAVALRY EQUIPMENT
Federal
Spurs

Cavalry issue, Type I (smooth surface)	$40 to $110
Cavalry issue, Type II, (stippled, rooster-neck pattern)	$50 to $115
Officer's with US cast on with side of neck	$400 and up

Stirrups

Artillery, brass, marked US on base	$85 to $175
Officer's, brass	$75 to $175
M–1859 enlisted man's, leather hooded	$200 to $300

Bits

US Cavalry	$100 to $275
Artillery, M–1863	$75 to $450
1860 cavalry officer's, gilded	$350 and up

Saddles

Grimsley	$1,100 and up
Jenifer	$900 and up
Officer's, brass-bound padded seat	$1,600 and up
M–1859 McClellan (standard issue)	$1,600 and up

Miscellaneous

Cruppers	$50 to $100
M–1859 McClellan saddlebags	$500 and up
M–1859 bridle and reins	$300 and up
Saddle holsters	$500 and up

Confederate

Spurs

Richmond pattern	$100 to $300
Mississippi pattern	$100 to $300
CS cast on either side of shank, matching pair	$2,500 and up

Stirrups

Richmond or Grimsley pattern, brass	$200 to $400
CS use with "C" bosses	$500 to $1,100
Tredegar pattern, brass	$200 to $350

Bits

CS Richmond	$250 to $500
CS use with "C" bosses	$500 to $110
Iron pattern CS bit, brass plated	$150 to $400

Saddles

CS version of McClellan with CS saddle shield	$2,100 to $4,000
CS Jenifer	$2,100 and up

Miscellaneous

Saddlebags	$500 and up

CERAMICS

Figurine. Lincoln on Horseback, Ca. 1880s. Staffordshire-type.

    "Abraham Lincoln" in raised letters $1,200 to $1,300

Mug. "Maj. Gen. Ulysses S. Grant." Ca. 1872.

    Transfer of Grant on obverse;

    Maj. Gen. Quincy Adams Gillmore $300 to $350

Pitcher. "Little Eva." Ca. 1860s. English ceramic. 8½" h.

    Shows slave sale on one side,

    Little Eva on the other $600 to $700

Vase. Abraham Lincoln. Ca. 1860s. Fenton Pottery,

    Bennington, Vt., oval with a relief of

    Lincoln bust $350 to $400

With the Stars and Bars of the Confederacy on high, a company of infantry moves up during the reenactment of the Battle of Shiloh. In reality, few rebel units looked this smart. If spit and polish were the deciding factor, the Confederacy wouldn't have lasted a month. (CT)

CORPS BADGES

The badge types listed here are metal pin-ons, although most corps badges also existed in cloth form. Most of the cloth badges, however, are sewn on caps and blouses and are not sold separately. Many metal badges are inscribed with the soldier's name, rank, and unit, and are so noted in this list as "I" for inscribed or "U" for uninscribed. The price range includes both excavated and nonexcavated badges.

1st Corps (circle or sphere)	I $500 to $700, U $325 to $475
2nd Corps (trefoil)	I $500 to $700, U $325 to $475
3rd Corps (lozenge)	I $500 to $700, U $325 to $475
4th Corps (triangle)	I $500 to $700, U $325 to $475
5th Corps (Maltese cross)	I $500 to $700, U $325 to $475
6th Corps (Greek cross)	I $500 to $750, U $325 to $475
7th Corps (crescent and star)	I $550 to $750, U $325 to $500
8th Corps (six-point star)	I $500 to $700, U $300 to $475
9th Corps (shield with anchor)	I $500 to $775, U $375 to $550
10th Corps (four-bastioned fort)	I $575 to $850, U $375 to $550
11th Corps (crescent)	I $525 to $700, U $325 to $475
12th Corps (five-point star)	I $450 to $750, U $325 to $500
14th Corps (acorn)	I $500 to $750, U $400 to $575
15th Corps (cartridge box, "40 rounds")	I $500 to $750, U $400 to $575
16th Corps (circle with cutouts)	I $450 to $750, U $400 to $550
18th Corps (cross with trifoliated arms)	I $500 to $700, U $375 to $525

EDGED WEAPONS

Knives

Federal

Bowie knife, inscribed	$800 and up
Hicks knife	$5,000 and up
Hicks knife with scabbard	$6,000 and up
Ames Rifleman knife	$1,600 and up
Ames Rifleman with scabbard	$2,500 and up

Confederate

Bowie knife, Confederate made	$750 to $2,000

General

Pocketknife, Sheffield made	$100 to $175
Bowie knife, Sheffield made	$30 and up
Bowie knife, Sheffield, large, 10-in. blade or longer	$1,200 and up
Bowie knife, same as above with scabbard	$1,600 and up

Pikes,

Federal

Marked naval boarding pike	$350 to $500
Lance from Rush's Lancer	$1,000 to $1,300
Lance from Rush's lancers with original pennant	$2,000 and up

Confederate

Pike made from bayonet	$250 to $500
"John Brown" pike	$800 to $1,500
Clover-leaf pike	$450 to $750
Lance with guidon or pennant still attached	$2,500 and up

Swords

Federal Army

Heavy cavalry saber, M-1840, stamped US, maker, and inspector, with scabbard	$450 to $650
Light cavalry saber, M-1860, stamped US, maker, date, and inspector	$400 and up
Dragoon, M-1833, Ames and US markings with scabbard	$500 to $750
Noncommissioned officer's sword, M-1840, stamped with US, maker, date and inspector, with scabbard	$300 to $400
Artillery officer's, M-1840, officer's hilt, etched blade, with scabbard	$2,750 and up
Staff and field officer's saber, M-1840, gilt guard, with folding counterguard, scabbard	$800 to $1,200
Foot infantry officer's saber, M-1850, etched blade with maker's name, with scabbard	$500 to $700

Federal Navy

Naval officer's cutlass, M-1860, brass basket with cutout USN, with scabbard with star on drag	$3,000 and up
Naval officer's saber, M–1852, etched blade with masker's name, with scabbard	$600 to $800

Confederate Army

Staff officer's with etched blade, Boyle & Gamble	$5,000 and up
Foot officer's with unetched blade, Boyle & Gamble	$1,500 to $2,000
Foot officer's with etched blade, Burger & Brothers	$5,000 and up
Staff/field, No. 1 open guard "CSA" under guard with etched blade, College Hill Arsenal, Nashville, Tenn.	$6,000 to $8,000

Foot officer's, unetched blade with firm name
and address, on top of scabbard mount,
James Conning, Mobile, Ala. $4,500 and up
Foot officer's with etched blade, E. J. John & Co.,
Macon, Ga. $5,000 to $7,000
Cavalry officer's saber, type with etched blade
and "CS" in oval guard, Leech & Rigdon,
Columbus, Miss. $14,000 to $16,000
1st Model cavalry with regimental markings,
Virginia Armory, Richmond, Va.,
modified prewar $1,500 to $3,000

EXCAVATED WEAPONS
Edged
Bowie knife $150 to $300
US cavalry sword $200 to $300
US saber bayonet $150 to $250
CS cavalry sword $400 to $700
CS staff officer's sword $400 to $700
CS saber bayonet $250 to $350

Firearms
Springfield rifle $250 to $375
Enfield rifle $250 to $375
Mississippi rifle $400 to $600
Spencer carbine $325 to $550
Colt revolver, .44 cal. $400 to $525
Starr Revolver $300 to $400

Weapon Accouterments

Bayonet, US	$50 to $80
Bayonet, CS	$125 to $275
Brass bullet mold	$75 to $250
Bormann fuse punch	$45 to $75
Gun tools	$5 to $15
Powder flask, military, complete	$125 to $150

FIELD GLASSES AND TELESCOPES

Naval telescope with markings	$700 to $1,200
Small cavalry 3- or 4-pull brass telescope	$100 to $275
Field glasses with case and strap with ID	$400 to $800
Field glasses with case and strap, military dealer mark	$275 to $375
Long, narrow design, telescopes at both ends, with ID	$350 to $750

FIREARMS

Longarms

Federal

M–1841 Mississippi rifle	$900 to $1,700
M–1855 rifle-musket	$950 to $1,350
M–1863 Springfield	$1,000 to 1,600
Remington Zouave	$1,000 to $1,400
Plymouth Navy rifle	$950 to $1,150
Henry rifle	$1,000 and up
Joslyn M–1862 carbine	$1,500 to $2,000
Sharps M–1863 carbine	$800 to $1,100
Spencer M–1860 carbine	$750 to $1,100

Confederate

Cook & Brother musketoon	$6,000 and up
Davis & Bozeman rifle	$9,000 and up
Fayetteville Armory rifle, standard	$4,500 and up
M–1841 Mississippi Rifle, Palmetto Armory	$6,500 and up
Morse carbine, Type I	$10,000 and up
Richmond rifled musket	$3,500 and up
Sharps-style carbine, government style	$4,250 and up
Tyler Texas rifle	$16,000 and up
Tarpley carbine	$32,000 and up

Handguns

Federal

Colt M–1849 pocket revolver	$400 to $900
Colt M–1851 Navy revolver, 1st model	$1,700 to $2,250
Colt M–1851, Navy revolver, 4th model	$775 to $1,200
Colt M–1860 Army revolver, standard	$800 to $1,300
Remington new Model Army revolver	$600 to $850
Starr .44 single-action revolver	$750 to $1,300

Confederate

Griswold revolver, 1st model	$8,000 and up
Leech & Rigdon revolver	$7,500 and up
LaMat revolver, 1st model	$8,000 and up
Spiller & Burr revolver, unmarked, 2nd model	$7,500 and up
Tucker, Sherrard & Co. revolver	$13,500 and up

The guidon of Company E, 2nd Massachusetts Cavalry, is typical of the guidons used in the war. When masses of cavalry fought in battles, such as Brandy Station, guidons helped identify individual units. Usually, troopers dismounted to fight, and the favorite weapon was the carbine. Sabers were mostly for ceremonial use. (USMA)

FLAGS
Federal

Civilian national flag, 33 or 34 stars	$600 and up
Infantry or artillery national color, with regimental designation painted or embroidered on center strip	$9,000 and up
Infantry regimental color, eagle in center	$10,000 and up
Cavalry standard with unit designation	$9,500 and up
Cavalry guidon	$1,500 and up
Artillery guidon, militia	$1,500 and up
Headquarters flag	$5,000 and up
Corps flag	$5,000 and up

Confederate

Battle flag, Army of Northern Virginia pattern	$30,000 and up
Battle flag, Hardee pattern	$20,000 and up
Battle flag, Van Dorn or Polk pattern	$20,000 and up
Swallowtail guidon	$3,500 and up

GLASSWARE

Bottle. Gen.George McClellan. 1864. Figural pedestal bust,
    mold blown glass. Black. 6" h. with opening
    on top of head $500 to $600
Mug. "Union Forever." 1870s. US
    clasped-hands motif $200 to $300
Tumbler. Civil War ordinance decoration,
    US 1860s. Cannon with grape,
    American flag with 234 stars $400 to $500
Wall Plaque. Abraham Lincoln. 1864. Milk glass.
    High relief bust centered in latticed
    pattern of split rails $450 to $500

A photograph in uniform taken at a local studio was part of the ritual of going to war. Posing here is the Reverend M. E. Smith, a chaplain in the Confederate army. Daguerreotypes of Civil War soldiers are popular with collectors today, particularly if the soldier is identified on the photograph. (NA)

INSIGNIA

Federal army (unexcavated)

Officer's Embroidered Headgear

Infantry hunting horn	$300 and up
Artillery crossed cannon	$300 and up
Cavalry crossed sabers	$400 and up
Mounted rifles trumpet	$500 and up

Enlisted Man's

Staff wreath	$75 to $125
Infantry hunting horn	$75 to $125
Artillery crossed cannons	$50 to $75
Cavalry crossed sabers	$75 to $125
Mounted rifles trumpet (M-1858)	$175 to $225
Irish Brigade hat wreath	$200 to $300
Regimental numbers and company letters	$10 to $25

Officer's Embroidered Headgear Devices (metal-backed)

Hardee hat eagle sidepiece	$175 to $350
Cavalry crossed sabers	$475 to $600
Engineer's castle/wreath	$550 to $800
Signal Corps crossed flags	$800 and up

Officer's Shoulder Straps (matched pairs)

Lieutenant general	$1,000 and up
Brigadier general	$400 to $700
Colonel	$350 to $600
Captain	$175 to $350

Shoulder Scales (matched pairs)

Enlisted scales	$200 to $300

Pictured is a soldier's sewing kit from the collection of enthusiast E. D. Simes. Civil War artifacts were being collected before the Civil War was over. Newspapers reported people scouring battlefields for guns and pieces of uniforms almost before the smoke had cleared. (CT)

Hat Cords

Infantry, blue, wool	$25 to $50
Artillery, red, wool	$25 to $50
Cavalry, yellow, wool	$50 to $100
Dragoon, prewar, orange, wool	$225 to $350

Confederate Army (unexcavated)
Officer's Headgear Devices (metal-backed)

South Carolina hat plate	$25 to $400
Louisiana hat plate	$400 to $600
Georgia hat plate	$250 to $400

KNAPSACKS AND HAVERSACKS

Knapsacks, Federal

Regulation tarred canvas knapsack	$75 to $150
Buchanan knapsack	$500 to $800
Joubert knapsack	$1,000 and up
Rider's tent-knapsack	$1,700 and up
Regulation US knapsack with soldier's ID painted on	$500 to $1,300

Haversacks. Confederate

Basic Confederate style	$1,700 and up

Haversacks, Federal

Black oilcloth	$700 to $1,100
Undyed canvas	$200 to $450
Leather	$250 to $500
Keech's haversack	$700 to $1,100

Leather Goods, Federal

Belts

M-1833 foot artillery sword belt, buff leather, eagle plate	$550 to $850
Federal infantry waist belt, bridle leather, US oval plate	$150 to $300
Federal infantry waist belt, with small US plate	$300 to $450
Federal light artillery sword belt, bridle leather, eagle plate	$775 to $850

Slings

M-1840 NCO sword sling, bridle leather	$275 to $350
Federal carbine sling, over-the-shoulder, black leather	$500 to $750
Federal musket sling, bridle leather	$350 to $550

Sword Frogs

M–1840 naval cutlass sword frogs	$50 to $100
M–1855 to M–1863, various sword bayonet frogs	$50 to $100

Holsters

M–1860 Colt holster	$300 to $500
M–1863 Colt or Remington holster	$300 to $500
E. Gaylord dragoon holster	$750 to $900

MEDALS AND TOKENS

Antislavery "Am I Not a Man and a Brother." Ca. 1850s.
    1¼" white metal. Kneeling slave praying.
    Reverse Golden Rule $75 to $100

Grant Peace Medal. 1871. Obverse: "Let Us Have Peace—
    Liberty, Justice, Equality" bust of Grant and peace pipe
    (312 struck of this silver medal) $2,500 to $3,000

Ku Klux Klan. Flags behind large burning cross.
    Inscribed "Onward Christian Soldiers."
    Round nickel finish $75 to $90

Service Medal. 1860s. Brass medal with ribbon
    or bar loop; embossed bust portrait of Lincoln,
    inscribed "With malice toward none.
    With charity for all." $150 to $175

Sumter Medal. 1861. 2½" bronze. Issued to Union
    officers and men who defended Ft. Sumter in April 1861.
    Bas relief profile of Gen. Robert Anderson, the fort's
    commander. Reverse depicts soldier raising flag $800 to $1,000

After a battle, their wounds bandaged, Confederate soldiers rest in the shade. These men are lucky to be alive. Military medicine was still in its infancy during the war, and many of the wounded perished from infections caused by unsanitary conditions in field hospitals. (NA)

MEDICAL EQUIPMENT

US army staff surgeon's capital operating case	$2,200 to $4,300
Large standard-size US surgeon's kit, with ID	$3,700 and up
CSA surgical kit, with ID	$3,500 and up
Large amputation kit	$200 to $3,000
Surgeon's capital operating kit	$3,000 to $4,500
Pocket surgical kit	$350 to $650
Metacarpal saw	$50 to $100
Bone file	$50 to $75
Straight forceps/bullet extractors	$175 to $225
Scarificator	$350 to $600
Surgical scalpel	$50 to $75
Medical knapsack	$1.000 to $1,750
Medical chest with original glass vials	$500 to $800
Apothecary jar	$125 to $200
Officer's whiskey flask, with ID	$350 to $550
Surgical practices textbook	$150 to $300
CSA *Manual for Military Surgeons*	$1,500 and up

MESS GEAR

Knives, all metal, wooden handle, and bone handle	$10 to $25
Forks, three-tined, metal, bone or wooden handle	$10 to $25
Spoons, metal, wooden and bone handle, folding-type	$10 to $25

Knife-Fork-Spoon Combinations

Two-piece combination bearing "Richards Patent of July 23, 1861"	$200 to $300
Robert's patent two-piece combination set	$150 to $250
Three-piece combination marked "Norman Ely & Co. Phila. Patent Feb. 4, 1862"	$175 to $275

Cups and Plates

Standard-issue tin cup, unmarked	$75 to $125
Standard-issue tin cup, but marked	$150 to $300
New England contract tin cup	$100 to $200

Mess Plates and Pans

Standard tin plate, varying from 8 to 9 inches in diameter	$50 to $100

MUSIC, SHEET

"Butler's Grand March." 1884. Lithograph of
    Greenback presidential candidate
    Gen. Benjamin Butler $50 to $75

"Gen. Grant's Quick Step." 1868. Beadle & Co.,
    Philadelphia. Bust portrait of Grant $50 to $75

"Battle Hymn of the Republic." 1862. Adopted to
    "Glory Hallelujah." Oliver Ditson & Co.,
    Boston $35 to $50

"Beauregard's Charleston Quickstep." Bust of
    Beauregard with crossed swords and laurels.
    J. C. Schreiner & Sons $35 to $45

"Dear Mother I've Come Home to Die." 1864.
    Firth, Son & Co., N.Y. $25 to $35

"Dixie's Land." 1861. Daniel Emmett $100 to $150

"Wanted/A Substitute." Lithograph bust of sad man
    "I'm Drafted," and bust of happy man "I Ain't" $35 to $50

"When Johnny Comes Marching Home." 1863.
    Henry Tomnan & Co, Boston. Cover design of type
    encased in a shield of stars, small illustration of
    military caisson $35 to $50

MUSICAL INSTRUMENTS

The prices indicate instruments in conditions ranging from fair to fine. Fine-condition instruments have no more than a few minor dents, no missing parts, no splits or cracks in tubing or surface metals, and slides and valves free of corrosion. Decorated drums are exceedingly rare and bring high prices, partly because they are coveted by both Civil War and folk art collectors.

Brass

Over-the-shoulder	$375 to $1,350
Upright	$300 to $850
Bell front	$300 to $900
Circular	$350 to $1,000

Bugles

Standard government issue of copper or brass, with manufacturer's name	$500 to $1,300
Brass double-twist bugle, unsigned	$300 to $400
British copper or brass bugle	$150 to $300

Fifes

Fife pitched in C, signed	$60 to $100
Fife pitched in B-flat, signed	$75 to $125

Drums

Snare drum, plain	$400 to $600
Snare drum, painted	$5,000 and up
Bass drum, plain	$400 to $750
Bass drum, painted	$5,000 and up

Collectors will see only the drums, not the drummers of the Rhode Island 2nd Infantry band. Decorated drums like these in good condition are among the most prized (and most expensive) of Civil War collectibles. (NA)

AUTOGRAPHS

Two prices are given below, respectively, for signatures of any date and for handwritten letters written during the war, complete with the signature of the writer. There is intense competition among collectors for letters written by Abraham Lincoln, Robert E. Lee, and Stonewall Jackson, and prices can vary wildly.

Abraham Lincoln	$3,000 and up, $8,000 and up
Ulysses S. Grant	$500 to $900, $3,000 and up
George Meade	$100 to $200, $400 to $800
George B. McClellan	$100 to $150, $500 to $1,000
George A. Custer	$2,000 to $2,500, $5,000 and up
W. T. Sherman	$350 to $700, $750 to $1,500
Robert E. Lee	$2,500 and up, $8,000 and up
Stonewall Jackson	$3,000 to $5,000, $9,000 and up
J. E .B. Stuart	$2,000 to $3,000, $7,000 and up
A. P. Hill	$1,250 to $2,250, $7,000 and up
John Mosby	$250 to $500, $5,000 and up
James Longstreet	$150 to $250, $4,000 and up

BOOKS

Books on the Civil War and related topics number more than 50,000, and prices vary with rarity, condition, and interest. First editions and books signed by the author are considerably more expensive.

Alexander, Edward Porter. *Military Memoirs of a Confederate.*
    New York, Charles Scribner's Sons, 1907. $45 to $60

Browen, J. H. *The Soldiers in Our Civil War,* Vol. I.,
    (A) Dias, Nov. 1894. $75 to $100

Longstreet, James. *From Manassas to Appomattox.*
    Philadelphia: 1903. $50 to $60

Evans, Gen. Clement Anselm. *Confederate Military History:*
    A Library of Confederate States History in 12 Vols.,
    Written by Distinguished Men of the South.
    1st Ed. Atlanta, Ga. Confederate Pub. 1899.
    Original cloth $650 to $750

Freeman, Douglas Southall. *Lee's Lieutenants: A Study*
    in Command, Manassas to Malvern Hill. 1st Ed.
    3 Vols. New York: Charles Scribner's Sons, 1942. $325 to $400

Grant, U. S. *Personal Memoirs of U.S. Grant.*
    2 Vols. New York, 1885. $100 to $150

Irby, Capt. Richard. *Historical Sketch of the Nottoway*
    Grays, Co. G, 18th Virginias, Garnett's Brigade.
    Signed inscription to Rev. J. W. Jones,
    fighting parson of 13 Va. Tipped–in
    albumen photos. $1,000 to $1,250

Mitchell, Margaret. *Gone With the Wind.* 1st Ed.
    1st Issue. New York: Macmillan. $1,800 to $2,000

Wallace, General Lew. *Ben Hur: A Tale of Christ.*
    1st Ed. 1st Issue. presentation inscribed $2,700 to $3,000

Stowe, Harriet Beecher. *Uncle Tom's Cabin, Or Life*
    Among the Lowly. 1st Edition, 1st issue.
    12 Vols. Boston: 1852. Original cloth. $7,000 to $7,500

Lincoln Titles

Anonymous Booklet. *Lincoln Catechism-Guide to Presidential Election of 1864.* Negro caricature on cover. Anti-Lincoln with pro-McClellan questions and answers. $75 to $100

Carpenter, Francis Bickness. *Six Months at the White House with Abraham Lincoln.*
New York: Hurd & Houghton, 1866. $65 to 75

Sandberg, Carl. *Abraham Lincoln: The Prairie Years.* 2 Vols,

_____. *Abraham Lincoln: The War Years.* 4 Vols. NY, 1939. $75 to $85

CURRENCY

Confederate

An acute shortage of coinage metal caused the Confederacy to rely almost solely on paper currency. (Confederate one-cent pieces, Liberty head, laurel wreath on reverse, uncirculated, are valued from $8,500 to $15,000.) Seven issues were produced during the war, totaling $1.5 billion. By war's end, Confederate paper money was worthless, as the government refused to redeem it. Uncirculated bills command the highest prices.

1861 Issue

Criswell–1. T–1. $1,000. 1861 Issue. Face design:
    Calhoun left, Andrew Jackson right,
    only 607 issued $1,500 to $2,500

Criswell–4. T–4. $50. Negroes hoeing cotton.
    $500 in discs. "Interest Half a Cent A Day" $600 to $1,250

Criswell–23–33. T–9. $20. Large sailing schooner
    in center, large "20" left $15 to $35

Criswell 99–100. T–17. $20. Black with
    green design, Ceres seated between
    Commerce and Navigation $45 to $90

1864 Issue

7th Issue. $10. Central vignette of "Field Artillery."
    More than nine million issued; most
    common genuine CSA note $3 to $5

DOCUMENTS

Confederate

Imprinted

Executive Department	$125 to $200
Signed by President Davis	$1,300 to $2,000
Cabinet departments (except Navy)	$75 to $125
Signed by secretary of department	$400 to $1,000
Navy	$200 to $400
Signed by secretary of navy	$500 to $850
Military broadsides, full-sheet size	$400 to $800
Military broadsides, half-sheet size	$200 to $350
Stock certificates of Southern companies	$175 to $250
Military commissions	$300 to $500
Confederate paroles for Union soldiers	$300 to $350
Oaths of amnesty or allegiance for Confederate soldiers	$75 to $175

Manuscripts

Soldier's letter with camp life or personal content	$25 to $50
Soldier's letter describing battles or historic events	$100 and up
Civilian letters describing historic events	$100 and up
Slave bills of sale, war dated	$50 to $100
Letters that came through blockade, with covers	$900 and up
Letters from Confederate POWs	$75 and up

Postage stamps

The prices below are for stamps in fine to very fine condition; the first price is for unused stamps, the second for used. Stamps on their original envelopes were worth at least a 100 percent premium.

1861, five cents, President Davis, green	$140, $90
1862, two cents, Andrew Jackson, green	$425, $500
1862, ten cents, Thomas Jefferson, rose	$650, $375
1862-64, five cents, President Davis, dark blue	$8, $15
1863, ten cents (frameline), President Davis, blue (shades)	$2,200, $1,000

War is a costly business, and the Union could outspend the Confederacy many times over. As the war dragged on, the Confederate government relied increasingly on bond issues to raise money to keep its armies in the field. As the bond certificates shown indicate, few were re-deemed. Genuine certificates carry authentic signatures and are prized by collectors. (MC)

NEWSPAPERS AND MAGAZINES

Antietam—Sept. 20, 1862—"The Great Victory."
  New York Times. ". . .[F]ull particulars from our
  special correspondent...vividly detailed
  accounts" $125 to $150

Fall of Atlanta. Sept. 19, 1864. *New York Daily Tribune.*
  8 pp. Front-page map $175 to $200

Fall of New Orleans. Oct. 17, 1861. *New Orleans
  Daily Delta.* Details about how
  the city was captured $1,100 to $1,200

Farragut Attacks CSA Positions at Mobile Bay.
  July 29, 1864. *Galveston Tri-Weekly News.* 2 pp.
  Direct report from Mobile Bay.
  Also outline of CSA's war aims $450 to $500

Stonewall Jackson Wounded at Chancellorsville.
  June 3, 1863. *Houston Tri-Weekly Telegraph* $500 to $600

Lincoln Assassination. April 17, 1865.
  Philadelphia Inquirer. 8 pp. All pages bordered
  in black. Large picture of John Wilkes Booth
  and map of escape route $100 to $125

The War Begins! April 27, 1861. *Harper's Weekly.*
  Report of bombardment of Ft. Sumter $100 to $175

Gettysburg—Horrible Realities of War
  Graphically Depicted in Brady Photographs.
  Aug. 22, 1863. *Harper's Weekly* $100 to $150

Bombard of Fredericksburg. Dec. 28, 1862.
  Harper's Weekly. Engravings of battle scenes $75 to $100

PAINTINGS, CARTOONS, AND OTHER ART MEDIA

Cartoons, Lincoln Related

"I Knew Him, Horatio, A Fellow of Infinite Jest."
  Pub. by Thomas Strong, NY, 1864. Opponent
  George McClellan, holds head of Lincoln.
  Gravedigger in background $400 to $450
"Man of Peace or War." 1861. Thomas Nast's
  two-panel view of Lincoln inauguration.
  Lincoln in robes titled "Peace"
  and in armor titled "War" $75 to $100
"Lincoln as a Monkey." David H. Strother (attrib.),
  1863. Monkey with Lincoln head on chair
  issuing Emancipation Proclamation to little man.
  Pencil on paper $125 to $150

Military and Other Political Cartoons

(Jeff Davis) Untitled. Anonymous, ca. 1870. Allegorical
  depiction of Davis sulking in doorway as Negro
  politician occupies his seat in Congress $75 to $100
"Grant Turning Lee's Flank." *Harper's Weekly*, 1963.
  Grant picks up Lee's coattails and gives him
  smack on backside with switch $125 to $150

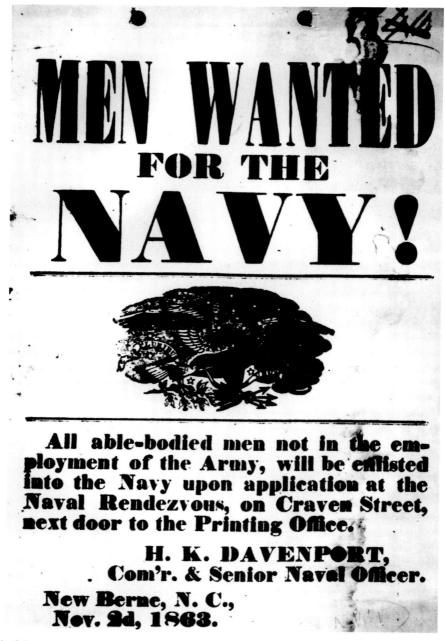

MEN WANTED

FOR THE

NAVY!

All able-bodied men not in the employment of the Army, will be enlisted into the Navy upon application at the Naval Rendezvous, on Craven Street, next door to the Printing Office.

H. K. DAVENPORT,
Com'r. & Senior Naval Officer.

New Berne, N. C.,
Nov. 2d, 1863.

Colorful recruiting posters are prized by collectors of Civil War ephemera and constitute a collecting field in itself. Posters are rare, and the variety is almost limitless. Placed in prominent places, they were directed to the local citizenry. Printed in small numbers, they were usually displayed for a few weeks at most. (NA)

Paintings

(The) "Color Sergeant." 1885. Watercolor gouache on
   brown paper. Signed Rufus Fairchild Zogbaum.
   5½ X 8¾" $2,500 to $3,000

"Gen'l George A. Custer." 1862. By "A.A. Frain, Artist."
   Oil half-length portrait. 24 X 34½" $20,000 to $25,000

"Skeletal Union Drummer." Ca. 1864. Unknown.
   Oil on canvas. Skeleton in Union uniform beats
   drum as fire and smoke curls around him.
   Possibly CSA origin. 8 X 12" $2,500 to $3,000

Miscellaneous Art Media

"Confederate Cavalryman." 1860s. Artist unknown.
   Graphite,charcoal and chalk drawing.
   17½X 21½" $300 to $350

"Kensaw (sic) Mt." Late 1860s. Primitive mixed media
   on wood depicting famous battle $1,100 to $1,200

"Gen. George B. McClellan." Charcoal drawing
   signed and dated by Katherine M. Baker, 1862 $1,000 to $1,200

PHOTOGRAPHS
Federal
Cartes de Visite

Head-and-shoulders pose	$10 to $20
Head-and-shoulders with subject identified	$25 to $45
Full-length pose, showing leather gear	$25 to $50
Full-length, with leather gear and musket	$50 to $85
Cavalryman with carbine	$200 to $300
Outdoor view of cavalryman and horse	$300 and up

Signed Images

George A. Custer	$7,500 and up
Ulysses S. Grant	$2,250 and up
W.illiam T. Sherman	$1,000 and up
George B. McClellan	$350 to $550
Ambrose E. Burnside	$300 to $450

Dealers and collectors meet at photo fairs around the country to buy and sell Civil War era images and equipment. Photographs of men in uniform and battlefield scenes are perennial favorites and command high prices. (GG)

The most popular photographic image of the Civil War era was that of Abraham Lincoln, shown here with his son Thaddeus. This image was widely reproduced by E. and H. T. Anthony & Co., and offered either individually or in assortments, and is found in many family albums of the period. (GG)

TIMEPIECES

Clocks

"Abraham Lincoln Mantle Clock." Ca. 1870. French works,
    unmarked. Metal with porcelain face. Figure of Lincoln,
    seated, with stack of books at feet. Clock supported
    by four figural turtles in each corner as feet $2,500 to $3,000

"Winfield Scott Hancock." 1880. Reverse painting on
    glass of Gen. Hancock on horseback. Wooden case with
    arched top and turned spires $1,000 to $1,300

Watches

Gen.(P.) T.G. Beauregard Pocket Chronograph.
    Made by L. B. Tuchman, Birmingham, England.
    Engraved, G. T. Beauregard, May 7, 1861.
    " With three stars. Awarded by Beauregard to
    David R. Jones. Inside cover engraved $5,000 to $6,000

Union Soldier's Pocket Watch. Ca. 1862. T.F. Cooper,
    London. Silver watch with chain. Face with painted
    illustration of soldiers holding flag, camp tents
    in background $1,600 to $1,750

TOYS AND GAMES

Mechanical Banks

"Artillery Bank, Confederate." Shepard Hardware Co.
Artilleryman in gray. Coin fired into tower.
Repainted $700 to $800

"Stump Speaker." Ptd. 1886. Black figure in top hat,
deposits coin in satchel $2,000 to $2,500

Still Banks

Gen. Benjamin Butler Frog Bank. 1884. J.&E. Stevens.
Caricature of Butler's frog holding
handful of greenbanks $1,200 to $1,500

Gen. Philip Sheridan on Prancing Horse. 1910-25 $200 to $250

"Abraham Lincoln Bust." 1920s. A. C. Rehberger $25 to $35

Games

"Battle of Gettysburg Wood Table to Game." 1880s.
Full-color litho on box. Bird's-eye view of battle $350 to $400

"Great American War Game." 1899. 25½ X 12" box
with foldout of battle scene, 22 metal soldiers
and two wooden cannons, steel balls $1,000 to $1,500

"Naval Engagement." McLoughlin Bros. 1870.
Separate board and pieces. 5½ X 9" box $75 to $100

Military Miniatures

"Camp on the Potomac." Haffner. 1880s. Display set
of 150 German 33-mm tinplate soldiers, flags,
pop-up tents with wood box $1,500 to $2,000

"Confederate Cavalry and Infantry." 1960s.
William Britains (English). Includes four
mounted troopers and infantry in action,
bugler, standard bearer, officer $375 to $400

Toys

Educational Myrioption, "Rebellion Story of
  Civil War." 1880. Color litho paper on wood.
  Scenes unfurl by turning knobs — $500 to $700
"Gettysburg Gun." Realistic wooden gun marked
  "Gettysburg, July 1, 2, 3, 1863. 10½" — $75 to $100

Three colonels of state militia strike poses suggesting that the conduct of the war is in good hands. Shown is the staff officer's weapon of choice—the pen. (NA)

UNIFORMS AND HEADGEAR
Federal
Officer's Uniform and Headgear
(Note: If a uniform is identified with the name of an officer, it will fetch a considerably higher price at auction.)

Frock coat, double-breasted, blue woo,l with original buttons:

General	$3,500 to $9,000
Infantry	$2,500 to $5,000
Cavalry	$3,500 to $6,500
Artillery	$3,000 to $5,500
Staff	$3,000 to $5,500

Frock coat, single-breasted, blue wool, with original buttons
and shoulder insignia:

Infantry and staff	$1,500 to $4,500
Cavalry	$3,500 to $6,500
Artillery	$3,000 to $5,500

Fatigue blouse (sack coat), four or five buttons, with or without shoulder insignia	$2,500 to $5,500
Officer's overcoat, sky blue wool, rank insignia on cuff, with or without cape	$2,500 to $5,000
Trousers, dark or sky blue wool with colored cord in seam for branch of service	$2,000 to $4,000
Hardee (Jeff Davis) hat, dark brown felt, branch insignia, eagle insignia with hat cord, plume	$7,500 to $13,000
Slouch hat with hat cord and branch insignia	$5,000 to $12,000
Forage cap, welted crown, with insignia	$3,500 to $7,500
Officer's kepi, chasseur trim or branch insignia	$2,500 to $7,500

Shown here are some regalia of war including frock coat and Hardee hat with plume and trousers of a first sergeant in the Corps of Engineers; swallowtail coat, breeches ,and Albert-style hat worn in a New York State Militia regiment; and, below, a modified Hardee hat worn in an Illinois Volunteer Infantry regiment with a bullet hole in the crown. (USMA)

Enlisted Man's Uniform and Headgear

Regulation-issue infantry or artillery frock coat with blue or red piping on collar and cuffs, nine-button front	$6,500 to $11,000
State-issue or private purchase frock coat	$4,000 to $7,000
Regulation-issue cavalry uniform jacket with yellow piping , 10- to 12-button front	$2,500 to $3,500
Regulation-issue fatigue blouse (sack coat)	$9,000 to $14,000
Regulation-issue dismounted overcoat	$3,000 to $6,000
Regulation-issue mounted overcoat	$6,000 to $8,000
Regulation-issue dismounted trousers	$9,000 to $14,000
Regulation-issue mounted trousers	$1,200 to $16,000
Regulation-issue fatigue cap	$1,200 to $3,750
1864 artillery shako with cords	$2,500 to $4,500

Confederate

Officer's Uniform and Headgear

Frock coat, double-breasted, with rank insignia and branch colors or collar and cuff:

Infantry	$20,000 to $35,000
Cavalry	$17,000 to $30,000
Artillery	$18,000 to $28,000
Staff	$18,000 to $28,000
Shell jacket, double- or single breasted	$11,000 to $27,000
Slouch hat, gray, tan, or black felt with insignia	$7,000 to $20,000
Kepi or forage cap, regulation	$8,000 to $20,000

Enlisted Man's Uniform and Headgear

Frock coat, single- or double-breasted	$15,000 to $35,000
Shell jacket, gray color, wool	$15,000 to $35,000
Slouch hat, gray, tan or black felt with insignia	$5,000 to $15,000
Kepi, butternut	$7,000 to $14,000

Major General George Meade's uniform and personal belongings included a buff silk general officer's sash, slouch hat, frock coat with insignia, Model 1839 topographical engineer officer's saber and scabbard, high-grade general officer's sword belt with gold bullion embroidery, dress epaulettes, a forage cap, boots, spurs, field glasses, and silverware from a general officer's mess kit. (CWM&L)

At a reenactment of the Battle of Shiloh, some latter-day Union officers take a moment to pose before a replica of a wall tent. In the actual battle, the Confederates struck at dawn, literally catching the Union army napping, and nearly carried the day. (CT)

Appendix E
BOOKS FOR CIVIL WAR ENTHUSIASTS

Two books produced and published by Time–Life Books are essential to the Civil War collector: *Arms and Equipment of the Union* and *Arms and Equipment of the Confederacy*. They are available in bookstores as a boxed set, which also includes the useful *Illustrated Atlas of the Civil War*. The boxed set is entitled *Arms, Equipment and Atlas of the Civil War*.

The *Official Price Guide to Civil War Collectibles*, compiled by Richard Friz and published in 1995 by the House of Collectibles in New York, will give a new collector an overview of what's being sold and for how much.

Also of interest to the collector are three books produced and published by Salamander, a British publisher, and reprinted in the United States in 1991 by Smithmark. Under the overall title *Rebels & Yankees*, the individual titles are *The Commanders of the Civil War*, *The Fighting Men of the Civil War*, and *The Battlefields of the Civil War*. The photography and illustrations are outstanding throughout. The editor of the series was Tony Hall; the technical advisor was Russ A. Pritchard, then the director of the Civil War Library and Museum in Philadelphia.

Another useful tool for the collector is the pioneering *Civil War Collector's Encyclopedia*, by Francis A. Lord. Originally published in 1964 in four volumes, the work has been reprinted in two volumes by The Black & Grey Press.

Collectors specializing in a particular field of the Civil War usually can find reference books to aid them. Most of these books share three characteristics. One, they are written by experts who explore their subject in depth; two, they are large-size paperbacks and well illustrated; and three, they are usually not found in conventional bookstores but in Civil War specialty stores. Examples include John D. McAulay's *Civil War Breech Loading Rifles,* published by Andrew Mowbray, Inc., of Lincoln, Rhode Island, and *An Introduction to Civil War Small Arms,* published by Thomas Publication,s of Gettysburg, Pennsylvania.

Many specialty books, now out of print, can sometimes be found in bookstores specializing in the Civil War. A number of the book dealers publish lists of their new acquisitions from time, and if you are interested, you should put your name on their mailing lists.